LOUISE on the LAM

A Foster Mom's Tale of Love, Rescue and a Tail on the Loose

ISBN 978-0-9897591-9-9
Printed in the United States of America
© 2015 by Sharon Cree
sharon@louiseonthelam.com
www.louiseonthelam.com

Illustrations by
Neil McMillin
Neillustrations

Cynthia A. Sudor, Publisher
1205 Ridge Road • Grantville, PA 17028
cynthia@caracynpublishing.com
www.caracynpublishing.com

All rights reserved. No part of this book may be reproduced or transmitted in any form or by any means, electronic or mechanical, including photocopying, recording or by any information storage and retrieval, without permission in writing from the author or publisher.

LOUISE on the LAM

A Foster Mom's Tale of Love, Rescue and a Tail on the Loose

by Sharon Cree

To Paul, Every tail has a tale! Sharon Cree

"Until one has loved an animal,
a part of one's soul remains unawakened."
— Anatole France

This book is dedicated to...

Ray, my loving husband, who has partnered with me in rescue and in life

Jessica, our daughter, whose accomplishments in life we are proud of (and also who scolds me when I have too many dogs at the house!)

Alicia, our daughter, Chris, her husband, and Tanner Ray, our first grandchild, whose beautiful family is more than any parents could ask for, and also for carrying on the love of the beagle breed

Barney, my first adopted beagle when I was a young college student, he was the reason I fell in love with that breed of dog

Nellie, our first family beagle-mix dog, who we lived with and loved for over 15 years

Louise, and all of our rescued and adopted beagles, for their courage and bravery in facing their life situations

Furry Friends Network volunteers and all rescue and shelter volunteers all over the world for giving their time, love, and patience to unwanted animals

Foster and adoptive parents of pets, for giving animals a loving home, and a second chance at the life they deserve

All the people mentioned in this book whose lives have been somehow touched by Louise

With great appreciation...

Without the supportive love of my husband, Ray, my work in rescue would not have been possible. Ray has partnered and stood beside me, saving and welcoming the many shelter dogs into our home. Most importantly, Ray never gave up in finding our Louise. He encouraged and urged me to write and share her incredible capture. "You need to finish your book," he'd suggest.

Thanks and appreciation extend to my Furry Friends Network comrades, particularly its co-founders Robin Scherer and Shawna Scherer, for bringing rescue beagles into my life. The perseverance and devotion these two ladies have for helping rescue dogs and cats is amazing. These two women are angels on earth. There are many more Furry Friends Network volunteers, too numerous to mention, who have become my extended family. We share a love for animals and all the facets of rescue that provide a cohesion and deep bond between us. Special acknowledgement goes to one of my beagle adopters and now a good friend, Melissa Flinn. She has worked tirelessly alongside me to fundraise and promote pet adoptions.

I am grateful to my sister, Denise Rush, whose plea for help so many years ago made me step into the world of rescue, a world that changed my life in a positive way forever.

It is important that I mention the unsung heroes of rescue work – the people involved in transports. Their efforts have brought foster dogs from many miles to me. They work behind the scenes and are a key element in rescue work.

In my early days of formulating this book, I attended writing workshops directed by Todra Payne. Todra taught me to "show and not tell" in my writing. She offered a creative flair and coached me to make my manuscript more descriptive.

On Louise's behalf, I need to recognize all the dedicated pet owners in this country, especially "parents" of special needs animals. Despite their issues or maladaptive behaviors, we have not given up on them. Whether it is a physical or a psychological problem, they have a safe haven and a forever home with us. "Kudos" to all the people who give their rescue pet a permanent residence.

With great appreciation, I thank Cynthia A. Sudor, CARACYN Publishing LLC, publisher of this book. Cynthia's positive feedback, overall vision, professional direction and guidance, know-how, enthusiasm and story editing made my first experience as an author truly enjoyable and rewarding. I will forever treasure our business and personal relationship.

My thanks also to the CARACYN Publishing team of Neil McMillin, Neillustrations, who illustrated the adventures in each chapter of this book and skillfully captured Louise and me in a caricature, to Randall Hughes, Viscul Creative, for his creative graphic design work, and to Sandra McGinnis, Global Copy Editing, for making sure the book flows grammatically.

Table of Contents

Tribute To Shelley, Ten Days of Love		1
Chapter One	Every Journey Starts with a Single Set of Paw Prints, Rescuing Riley	7
Chapter Two	Choosing Louise, Long Distance Love	17
Chapter Three	Be Careful What You Ask For	25
Chapter Four	Louise's Newest Adventure	31
Chapter Five	Good-bye to Our Nel Nel	45
Chapter Six	Relentless Rehabilitation	55
Chapter Seven	Rehabilitation Reinforcement	65
Chapter Eight	Bringing Home the Bacon	71
Chapter Nine	Louise on the Lam	87
Chapter Ten	Louise is Lost	99
Chapter Eleven	On the Lookout for Louise	111
Chapter Twelve	Operation Louise	125
Chapter Thirteen	The Stage is Set	139
Chapter Fourteen	Big Booms Home and Away	153
Chapter Fifteen	Aloha Louise!	175
Chapter Sixteen	Aloha Hawaii!	189
Chapter Seventeen	Louise Becomes a "Cree-gle"	201
Chapter Eighteen	Life with Louise Today	209
Chapter Nineteen	Reflections on Louise's Impact on My Life	221

My Life in Rescue Work with Furry Friends Network	231
Letter from Dolly, a Foster Beagle, on Her Way to Her New Forever Home	237
A Message from Furry Friends Network Co-Founder, Robin Scherer	238
Furry Friends Network Facts	240
Rescue and Shelter Facts	243
Bibliography	244
About the Author	247

Tribute to Shelley
Ten Days of Love

  A small sweetheart of a beagle captured my affection in the summer of 2003. Even though I fostered a few dogs before Shelley came into my life, she stole my heart. Like most rescue dogs, Shelley had a tough time of it before I fostered her. She was neglected, filthy, and overbred when I first met her. Her nails were curled and untrimmed. Her neck had a huge raw spot from the chain rubbing against her skin. But through all of the physical signs of neglect, there was a sweetness that shined through her. Maybe it was those soulful, brown, buggy eyes that looked right through you, from the warmth of her heart, despite her difficulties, into your heart. Shelley's eyes were dripping with a love I could not resist.

Shelley was a tri-color, dainty little beagle that needed a new lease on life. Ours was supposed to be a foster relationship. I would give Shelley a better life until she found a forever home. That is the way fostering a dog works.

Shelley was on a list of dogs on "death row" in a rural shelter in West Virginia. Before the shelter took her in, she had been running loose as a stray with a younger dog, probably her pup. The shelter consisted of six outdoor kennels where all the dogs were kept. Space was extremely limited. On a muggy Friday in August of 2003, I drove the hour and a half from the Harrisburg, Pennsylvania area to Baltimore, Maryland to meet the transport and pick up my new foster dog. This was arranged through the Furry Friends Network rescue group in central Pennsylvania.

When I arrived, I learned that the shelter had spayed Shelley while she was in heat. Because there had been no other place to house her, the dog warden had put Shelley in a night holding pen along with another dog. When the shelter workers realized the next morning that she was in heat, they feared Shelley had become impregnated. An appointment to have her fixed was promptly made. It is not uncommon to alter animals immediately before they are shipped out. However, I soon learned that performing this operation on a dog in heat can cause deadly complications.

Shelley was the dearest little thing in the whole world. She was no problem to have in the house and had no behavior issues. In fact, Shelley was peaceful and quiet. When

I first brought her home, I noticed that she was not getting up and around very often. This was maybe due to her recent surgery. She must be sore and needs rest, I reasoned.

On Monday, three days after Shelley arrived home with me, she developed an abscess at her incision site. We called the vet immediately and my husband, Ray, and I rushed her there. The vet is a twenty-five minute ride from our home in the country in Dauphin, PA, and we knew we had to get there quickly. The vet examined Shelley and then gave her an injection, drained the abscess, and prescribed antibiotics. *This is a relief*, I thought. *We treated this medical problem right away.* The abscess was probably the reason Shelley was so reserved and sullen.

Each day Shelley became stronger and more active. When I petted her, she looked at me as if to say, *Is this what life should really be like?* Shelley had never received love or attention. Being in a home and having loving human companionship was a new experience for her. Shelley learned to go for walks, ride in the car, play with toys, and interact with my dogs. I could just tell she was thinking, *Hey, life is pretty good!*

Never again would she be disregarded, living life on a chain. She was getting a much-deserved second chance. Those expressive eyes now penetrated me with warm appreciation. My husband, Ray, and I wanted to adopt Shelley. In the short time we had Shelley, our love for her grew each day and we wanted to make her a part of our family.

Then ten days after Shelley entered our lives, the unexpected happened.

At 2:00 a.m. I awoke with a jolt. Something was wrong. I could feel it. I looked down at the bed and saw Shelley in a pool of blood. All the blood clots on my bedspread were a horrific sight. What was happening?

Shelley was hemorrhaging, but she just lay there wagging her tail at me. Immediately, I ran to the phone and called a local vet's office that was open all night for emergencies. The vet was already in surgery and could not see us. Desperately, I phoned every animal hospital in our area, only to be disappointed by a pre-recorded message informing me the office was closed, and then, a glimmer of hope.

Finally, I found an all-night vet clinic forty-five minutes away. It was a long shot, but we were willing to do whatever we could to save Shelley. Cradled in a blanket that I quickly threw around her, I rushed to the car with Shelley in my arms. My husband sped at eighty miles an hour along dark and desolate roads to reach our emergency destination.

"Drive faster!" I cried from the back seat. "We're losing her!"

Shelley's gums were turning white. All the while, she never whined or whimpered. She simply looked at me during the entire car ride and feebly wagged her tail.

After Shelley was examined, the news was not good. Shelley had major internal problems from the spaying. We weren't concerned with the expense. We were prepared to spend whatever it cost to save our precious girl. But in the end, Shelley would have endured severe, permanent physical problems. She would be destined to a life of pain and discomfort, chronic infections, and urinary tract problems. She had already lost so much blood. We made the irrevocable decision to say our painstaking good-byes. We had Shelley euthanized.

Ten days. That is all the time we had to fall in love with this sweetheart of a beagle and then say good-bye to her.

Alerting Furry Friends Network rescue group and my rescue contacts was painful. Shelley had made such a good impression on all of them…her sweetness, her welcome acceptance of the love we lavished on her. More information about Shelley's background poured in to me…more of her sad story. Many people mourned for Shelley, none of them more than my husband, Ray, and I.

For the next two years, I was literally a basket case. I cried for months, obsessing over her death. *Why did this happen? Couldn't I have had her just a little longer? This wasn't fair - to Shelley or to me.* I wanted to get out of rescue, it was too much work, too much heartache. It's not worth putting one's self through this anguish. My only small comfort was that Robin Scherer, the executive director and co-founder of the Furry Friends Network, reassured me that the ten days Shelley spent with Ray and me were the best of her life. If a dog departs being loved, that's all that matters. No matter what was said to me, I could not be consoled. The sadness was more than I thought I could bear.

As time went on, instead of distancing myself from rescue and foster work, I decided to snap out of it and turn this painful, horrible, negative event into something positive. No more wallowing in my sorrow. I made the decision that it was time to step up to the plate again.

One at a time, I would save more dogs like Shelley . . . dogs that were unwanted and forgotten, used only for breeding and hunting . . . hounds that were discarded and viewed as disposable when they became too old to have litters or could not run fast or for so many other ridiculous reasons. I made the decision that I wanted to offer love to dogs who'd never had any form of affection in their lives. Shelley did not die in vain.

Even though she was considered our foster dog, we paid more than one hundred dollars for Shelley to be cremated privately. We wanted what was best for her. We wanted her to die with dignity and to honor her.

Shelley's ashes remain in a beautifully carved wooden box that sits on the fireplace mantle in our home. Although I thought about having a burial ceremony with neighbors and the few people who knew her in the short ten days she spent with us, I decided not to bury Shelley. She will stay where she belongs, inside our home with us.

Shelley is at home and at peace.

This book is dedicated to Shelley and to all the Shelleys out there.

This book is about another one of my foster dogs, Louise, whom I would have never met if I had not decided to continue my foster work.

Louise, you'll see, is a whole different experience…a real character…this is quite a real life dog tale that I know you will enjoy!

Chapter One

Every Journey Starts with a Single Set of Paw Prints

Rescuing Riley

"Hey, Sharon, can you help us out? Sally has thirteen puppies in her garage," begged my younger sister, Denise Rush. Her S.O.S. beckoned on a Friday morning in June

2002. Little did I know at that time that this one phone call would stir an adventure in my life that continues to this day. After that day, my world would be forever changed.

The timing was not good…as a teacher, with the school year just ending, I had scheduled some much-needed projects around the house. Painting our screened-in back porch was first on my list. My husband, Ray, a self-employed welder, works long hours. Most mornings, Ray leaves before sunrise and doesn't return until late in the evening. Home improvements, however, are my forte.

For a few moments, I was silent while I weighed my options. On the one hand, the porch had been neglected for an entire winter and needed dire attention. On the other hand, thirteen puppies were a handful for anyone, so I could understand Denise and Sally's dilemma.

"I'll be right over," the words spilled out of my mouth. *I guess I made my decision*, I thought, half way in disbelief.

My sister, Denise, and I are both animal lovers. Denise is a dog groomer. She had recently joined a newly formed animal rescue group called Furry Friends Network. Just a few weeks prior to this, one of her customers had informed her about this new organization that provided foster homes for countless dogs and cats that needed them. Denise could not resist getting involved as a volunteer even though she already had two cats and a yellow Labrador named Jada. Jada was a rambunctious playmate for my own beagle-mix, Nellie.

These thirteen puppies that were brought to Sally's home were marked "urgent" on "the list." That meant one thing for them…doomsday if they did not get fostered and then adopted. Sadly, as we know, most shelters euthanize animals due to lack of space, lack of adoption and lack of funding. Most weekends, Sally Cammack, at that time a Furry Friends Network volunteer, made the seven-hour trip to Mason County Animal Shelter, West Virginia and back again, herself. She saved all of the dogs that she could by loading them up in her car or van.

Now I found myself agreeing to help them out that summer while I was not teaching. I would have more time to devote to an energetic, squirmy and mischievous little puppy. *What was I getting myself into?* I wondered as Denise and I drove to Sally's home. It would not be long until I got the answer to my question.

When we arrived and opened the garage door, the scene was like a child's playground, except all the bubbly "kids" were "puppies"! Denise and I were up to our ankles in thirteen wet-nosed yelping puppies of all shapes, sizes and colors. These little bundles of pure energy were running, playing, skidding into each other and rolling around with their newly found freedom. You get the picture! Immediately, I was attacked like I was a new playmate or a new toy…all thirteen little fur balls ran to me and tugged at my shoelaces. It was impossible not to laugh out loud and be overwhelmed at the same time.

Eyeing the thirteen puppies of all mixes and matches of breeds, I spied a floppy-eared beagle-mix. I have a soft spot for beagles because of my love for my own beagle-mix, Nellie. This puppy was marked with what looked like a dark furry "mask" on his face. I was hooked!

Bouncing around near this beagle-mix was a yellow Labrador puppy that reminded me of Jada, my sister's yellow Lab. Thinking that this little golden fuzz ball would make a good playmate for the beagle-mix puppy, I informed my sister that I would foster these *two* puppies from Sally's garage.

Did I just say that out loud? I thought. *Two puppies!*

Driving home with these two puppies in my car, I knew I was headed into an entirely new life adventure. Suddenly, painting the porch could wait. This was an important job to do; it involved the lives of two dogs. I felt good about helping in this way, and pleased to be a part of new lives for at least two of these puppies.

What was I getting myself into? I wondered, yet again.

I soon found out that I was a bit unprepared as I stumbled into the world of rescue!

The next several days were a nightmare! I didn't have a clue about fostering rescue dogs. The puppies did not come with step-by-step instructions! And to make matters worse, I never had two puppies to take care of at once. For one thing, I had forgotten how often they peed…and for another, they peed *whenever* they wanted, *wherever* they wanted! But, there was a whole lot more that was different from the puppies that I had previously raised.

Rescue dogs tend to have heightened health issues because of their neglect. Poor nutrition and low body weight, skin conditions such as mange and ear infections are common, but treatable. I had to be on the fast track to quickly learn which medications are given for a slew of different parasites. Kennel cough and upper respiratory infections are frequent…and contagious. I had a steep learning curve to deal with fostering these two puppies. And, I had to learn fast. These two puppies had parasites and slight kennel cough when they arrived, so I had to administer medicines provided by the rescue to clear those up. It was up to me to make sure these two puppies would get a clean bill of health. Furry Friends Network rescue volunteers were with me every step of the way.

Little did I know at the time, as it would turn out, these were the first two foster dogs of many that I would become involved in helping. Saving the lives of these dogs and dogs like them, and paving the way for their adoptions, was to become a part of my life.

Despite the challenges, I was determined to honor my commitment to my sister, the rescue organization…and, most importantly, to these two wonderful puppies who had been on the "urgent list" and needed my love and attention. They were alive and I was going to make sure that they were on their way to better health as well. These puppies would be fostered by me, and then they would be placed in their forever home…that was always the plan with foster and rescue groups like Furry Friends Network.

When Ray came home that evening, he immediately got involved in naming the beagle-mix puppy. We named him Riley. Then we named the yellow Labrador puppy Daisy.

Daisy was already a "lucky dog." She had people interested in adopting her. Since the people who were interested in adopting Daisy were on a short vacation, I was fostering Daisy until they returned. Daisy, as it turns out, had a good temperament and was mild mannered. Riley, however, was another story all together. Our first foster dog turned out to be quite a challenge!

Riley, our new furry tenant, tormented Nellie, our beagle-mix, by constantly nipping her hind legs and ears, like any puppy might do. Riley was relentless. Nellie, now age twelve, preferred to snooze in the sun and not be bothered by a naughty little aggressive puppy. This had to be resolved so that Nellie could live in peace…so that we could *all* live in peace!

Riley, it turned out, even at eight weeks old, was showing classic alpha-male tendencies…even with people. Riley growled and refused to be cuddled when we picked him up. Instead of being a playmate with Daisy, the yellow Labrador puppy that would soon be in an adopted home, Riley snarled at her like a bobcat. It seemed like he wanted to eat Daisy alive. I had to keep Riley and Daisy separated. This was not what I had in mind! Riley was just plain nasty.

Something about Riley's eyes made everyone comment about them.

"He looks like a little demon," my mother-in-law whispered to me. I had to agree with her.

"He has devil eyes," my daughter said only half-jokingly. Once again, I had to nod in agreement.

Riley's "masked markings" around his eyes resembled Cleopatra. He looked like he was wearing heavy eyeliner. It gave his eyes a fiendish, sinister appearance. Sadly, Riley was living up to the image of those devilish "masked markings."

There were more challenges to come.

At his first check-up, the vet gave Riley the "stare test." The "stare test" is a nonverbal exercise to see who breaks the stare first, the vet or the dog, in this case, Riley. That would establish who was the alpha, the dominant one. The vet sat Riley on the table and she stared directly into Riley's eyes with an authoritative posture. A puppy usually turns away from that stare, to show submission. A minute passed. Two minutes passed. The tension mounted as the young woman vet stared at Riley…and the strong-willed Riley, at eight weeks of age, stared right back at her. Riley did not flinch, let alone blink. Riley, if he could talk, and in a way he was communicating through his actions, was saying, *Look, Lady, get this straight…I'm in control here!* As I watched this phenomenon as a bystander in the room, I thought at one point that Riley's devilish eyes were about to turn glowing red to match his reputation! The vet blinked first…she said she never saw this strong alpha behavior in a dog that young.

Desperate for more opinions, I took Riley over to my sister Denise's home about a week later to get her view on his unusual behavior. Denise was more used to handling different breeds in her grooming shop and perhaps she could lend some insight.

"What's wrong with Riley?" Denise said, shaking her head when Riley snarled at her when she picked him up. "I've never had a cute little, eight-week-old puppy act like this."

So, Denise was of no help in solving Riley's attitude challenge. She was just as surprised as I was.

Two weeks later, determined to find out more about Riley's behavior, I invited my friend, Betsy, over to my home to observe Riley. Betsy owned a 130-pound Rottweiler named Zeus. I figured that gave Betsy some credibility with "big attitude" dogs. Carefully, I brought Daisy, the eight-week-old, furry yellow Labrador puppy that I was temporarily fostering, in to interact with Riley. That barely lasted a minute. Riley immediately bared his teeth, flared his nostrils, bristled up his fur and became vicious. Riley lunged for Daisy like a greyhound bounding from the starting gate of a big race. Immediately, I rescued Daisy and removed her to her safe room once again.

Betsy shook her head. She was also baffled. Her Rottie, Zeus, never acted like this! She could offer no words of wisdom and wished me luck.

At this point I was desperate to control Riley. I delved into training manuals and studied ways to be the alpha. I learned that much of a dog's behavior is based on hierarchy of the group or herd. Dogs descend from wolves and the "wolf mentality." Educating myself how to become the calm and assertive "leader of the pack,"[1] I was going to figure out one way or another, what made Riley "tick."

All that education started to work. Little by little, Riley began to mellow and become easier to handle and even more likable overall. With positive reinforcement training, his aggressive behavior towards other dogs lessened. Using obedience commands, I made progress. His interaction with Nellie improved also, thank goodness.

Four weeks later, when Riley was just over twelve weeks old, Denise saw him again and remarked in a positive way, "Sharon, what did you *do* to this dog?"

My effort to show Riley who was in charge was working! I was now the alpha of our little "pack."

Over a short period of time, Riley grew into our hearts. I was proud of his improvement. Riley was my first foster dog and it was hard to give him up. Despite

---

[1] Cesar Millan, Cesar's Way, The Natural Everyday Guide to Understanding & Correcting Common Dog Problems, pages 68 – 73.

Riley being the little stinkpot that he originally was, Ray and I adopted him when he was five months old and welcomed him into our "forever home."

It turned out that my sister's, Denise's, desperate phone call to me that early June day was the beginning of a new chapter in my life…my life in animal rescue. At the time, I had no idea how much it would impact my existence. Rescue work over the last thirteen years has not only affected my life, but so many other lives…both four-legged and two-legged.

Growing up in Harrisburg, Pennsylvania, and spending summers with my cousin in Frackville, what is known as the "coal regions" of Pennsylvania, there was nothing that showed early signs of my getting involved in animal rescue work as an adult. During my childhood, pet dogs and cats were easily found in "free to a good home" ads or acquired through friends. As a youngster, the middle child of three girls, I had two dogs. The first one was a black and white terrier named Chi Chi and the other was a pedigree Siberian Husky named Nikki, with one blue eye and one brown eye. As a young girl I begged my father to buy Nikki for me, and he did. On walks, Nikki was strong and dragged me, who was small and thin, down the street as if I was a dogsled, but I was so happy to have her as a pet.

As an adult, living off-campus while in college at Penn State Middletown Campus to earn my teaching degree, I adopted a beagle named Barney at a local shelter. When I moved on to less expensive housing on campus, I could not take him with me. It was a hard decision for me. Working only part-time and being a full-time student, finances were tough. I had to find Barney a good home, and I did, often visiting him and the family who now owned him. Barney was quite a character and the family always had amazing stories to tell me about things he would do. Owning Barney was the beginning of my love for the beagle breed.

Now, as an adult and a third grade teacher, I was happily married to Ray, with two daughters grown and leaving us "empty nesters." One beagle-mix already in our home, Nellie, completed our family. Entering into the picture of my life, through my sister, Denise, was Riley, the Furry Friends Network, and rescue work.

Riley and many of my foster beagles have touched my life deeply.

But, as the story in this book will show you…no dog has ever affected my life as much as Louise!

Beagle Bit

"Beagle" is derived from the French word "begle" which in turn comes from the medieval "Begueule" meaning "gape throated." This probably refers to their baying. The Celtic word "beag" means "small."

Chapter Two

Choosing Louise

Long Distance Love

She looked so SCARED. Yep, that's exactly how it was spelled out on her website description: S-C-A-R-E-D in capital letters. She was one of two beagle sisters, Thelma and Louise. These two "scaredy-cat" dogs were hardly the dynamic duo that we identify with from the movie. It was thought that these two sisters, approximately aged one to two years, were never held or knew human touch. They were in a poor, rural, high-kill shelter in West Virginia that Furry Friends Network regularly assisted. Volunteers from the Furry Friends Network often made the seven-hour drive from central Pennsylvania to West Virginia delivering van-fulls of pet food, blankets, medical supplies, and cleaning products to this impoverished facility. Many shelters all across America are just getting by and need your help. If you can't volunteer, consider looking at your local shelter's "wish list" on their website and donating supplies.

In fact, my husband, Ray, and daughter, Alicia, and I witnessed firsthand the inadequate conditions there when Furry Friends Network organized a fixer-upper weekend in the fall of 2005. A group of us made the red-eye truck trip to West Virginia on a Friday afternoon. Eager to make repairs, we hauled tools, bathroom fixtures, and tons of dog kibble in our truck. Sally Cammack and another Furry Friends Network volunteer accompanied us in her van, toting a trailer overstocked with dog food. Pulling too much weight on the mountainous roads in West Virginia, Sally's transmission in her van blew up. Broken down, our weekend get-away turned disastrous. But Ray came to the rescue! Ray purchased a hitch for his truck, hooked up the trailer, and we all resumed the trip, leaving Sally's van to be towed and fixed at a nearby garage. Sally and the other volunteer squeezed into another car amongst the provisions we were transporting.

The caravan, with one less vehicle due to the transmission problem, arrived in West Virginia at about 2:00 a.m. We were exhausted. Later on Saturday morning, things looked brighter. Ray welded broken kennel locks, patched a leaky roof, and replaced a leaky faucet. Our daughter, Alicia, and I swept cobwebs and gave the shelter a fresh coat of paint. Alicia bent over a bathtub the rest of the day and washed the dogs so they would arrive in their foster homes clean-smelling. Sally operated a yard sale to raise funds for the shelter while another volunteer assembled special orthopedic off-the-floor chew-proof dog beds so the dogs would not have to sleep on the concrete. Tired and sweaty at 6:00 p.m., we called it a day. Despite our bad start, we were proud of our accomplishments. We departed for Pennsylvania early on Sunday morning with a cargo full of dogs emancipated from the confines of cages and moving onward to a new life.

These were the lucky ones that made it out. Shelters all across America are screaming for help. The plight of homeless animals in our country is a national disgrace. The statistics are alarming. Estimates range from four up to eleven million dogs and cats that are unwanted each year…yes, you read that correctly, *each year*. More than half are euthanized. These animals do not have a voice in meeting their demise. Only 12% of pets adopted come from shelters.

This shelter in West Virginia was no different. Pregnant momma dogs were dumped in a night bin by irresponsible owners. Regulations mandated by the county ordered the gassing of animals to keep numbers down. Unfortunately, only one out of every ten dogs in America ever gets a home. Backyard breeders produce excess litters, thinking only of the almighty dollar. Pet overpopulation is controlled by euthanizing able-bodied, healthy animals. This was the path that Thelma and Louise were quickly heading down. They could easily become another sad statistic.

Conditions at Thelma and Louise's shelter were not favorable. This shelter could barely afford the basic necessities. On top of kennels bursting at the seams and a shortage of food, the shelter operated without heat for almost three years. Mother Nature was not kind, either. Snow came early in the fall months of West Virginia's mountainous terrain. The animals, already in poor health, often got sick in the cold winter conditions. Volunteers worked diligently hosting fundraisers such as bake sales and "dog washes." Their hard work raised enough money to install a new heating system.

Just as things were looking up, the unthinkable happened around Thanksgiving Day, 2005. Due to a gas leak when the shelter was having work done and heating repairs were being made to the facility, the shelter exploded like a volcano. Fireballs swept through the facility in a matter of seconds. Meowing kittens were trapped in cages. Whining puppies had nowhere to run. Workers risked their lives and scrambled to open locked kennels to free the animals. The shelter burned to the ground. Unbelievably, all the animals made it out alive. But, many of those that did escape got singed and needed emergency medical care. Tumult and chaos erupted.

I will never forget reading the emails that Friday morning after Thanksgiving. "Animal Shelter in Ruins, Mason Fire – Warning, Graphic Pictures." I sat at my computer sobbing. The pictures were shocking. All that was left were charred remains of the shelter. Fortunately, the employees were unscathed, but the workman doing the repairs suffered severe burns. All the animals that managed to scurry to safety were now facing a bigger problem. Where would they live until a new shelter was built? A local farmer offered his land. Thelma and Louise, and other animals, would be housed in hog pens outside in the snow. Thelma and Louise were some of his first boarders from that burned down shelter. Now more than ever, Furry Friends Network needed to increase its rescue efforts.

Through my tears, I studied the image of the terrified, bewildered look on Louise's face on my computer screen. She looked even more scared than before…she was pathetic. You'd have thought Louise had seen Frankenstein. She appeared odd and peculiar looking, yet intriguing. I am not usually drawn to the red and white copper-nosed beagles. Thelma and Louise looked alike except that Louise had an unusual marking on her right ear. It looked like someone threw a splotch of white paint on it. Her red and white patterned fur resembled a Pinto horse.

Checking Louise's website picture on my computer night after night, I hardly concentrated on my schoolwork and ignored housework. I contemplated bringing Louise as another foster into my house. Normally, I prefer the tri-color beagles whose markings are distinct and brilliant: the black, brown, and white ones that are strikingly handsome and clearly defined. I call them "beagley-beagles." The website listed several of these. One by one I scrolled down and examined their grainy pictures. So many to help. So many that needed saved. Eight hundred dogs and cats are put to sleep every hour in our country…*every hour*. At least Louise would be one less.

When I choose a dog to foster, I get an instant connection to its picture. Something clicks. I feel an immediate attraction to the dog as though it is already mine. I just know that it will do well at my house. There was something about Louise that sparked my interest. She looked more scared than Thelma. Those headlight eyes of Louise's lured me.

But now was not the best time to get a foster dog. Our beloved beagle-mix, Nellie, was fifteen and in ailing health. X-rays revealed a large, inoperable tumor on her right lung. The prognosis was not good. Her aging face, weight loss, heavy breathing, reduced eating, and sagging eyelids indicated the end was near. I needed to focus on Nellie and enjoy the time that she had left with us.

Despite Nellie's grave condition, Louise's photo haunted me. I only knew that she was "scared," not much information to go on. The website offered no data on her temperament or disposition. Even her age was an approximation at possibly one to two years old. This is something that I am used to. I am often given little insight into my fosters' habits or personalities. Sometimes I am told the bare basics, such as "stray" or "owner surrender." That's not much to work with. With a new foster, I must address medical needs, socialization, housetraining, possible food aggression, or other situations that arise. It is important that I know if the foster dog gets along well with other dogs. My own dogs must accept a new foster coming onto their turf. Sometimes, adding one more "fur-kid" in the mixture changes the whole dynamics of the pack and disrupts my domestic harmony. Returning the dog to the shelter, as most people can do, is not an option for me. I made a commitment to save this dog's life. However, all my beagles, even Riley, with some training, have been great little dogs and I often wondered why they were given up in the first place. Most people complain they don't have the time or have chosen the wrong breed for their lifestyle. Perhaps a child became allergic or the puppy nipped the baby. Frequently, there are behavior issues, such as being too rambunctious or destructive, which can be workable. If a lifetime commitment could be made to the dog, shelters would not be so overcrowded.

Christmas vacation of 2005 arrived. I welcomed ten days off to catch up on chores around the house and spend time with Nellie and our two other dogs, Riley, now three years old, and our other beagle, BuddyLee, age three, whom we adopted in 2004. Moreover, I needed some rest and relaxation from my teaching responsibilities that included twenty-five third graders who were wound up for the holidays. Every time I want to take a break from fostering, I see another dog in need that tugs at my heartstrings. Sometimes I could kick myself because I don't take any time for me. A friend who adopted a beagle from me stated it very well when she described me as, "Fostering is in your blood, Sharon." And, that is true.

I hesitated showing my husband, Ray, the photograph of Louise. He often advised me, "You can't save them all, Sharon," when he observed all the work a foster dog poses at first. He knew I deserved some leisure time due to my hectic days at school as well. But I reckoned I could save Louise and make a difference in her life. Besides, I reasoned with myself, Louise can't start the New Year in a hog pen in the cold, wet snow.

Finally, making my decision, I emailed Robin, the co-founder and executive director of Furry Friends Network, to let her know that I wanted to foster Louise. She responded that another foster mom had already put in for both sister dogs, Thelma and Louise. She questioned my offer to foster as she knew that my beagle-mix, Nellie, was in frail health.

For a moment, I almost recanted, thinking that Louise would still be saved by the other foster mom. Talking to myself, I realized that maybe I had put my heart ahead of my brain. But Louise needed me. Somehow deep inside of me, I knew that. Besides, I had three years of fostering under my belt. With all those years and experience fostering, I considered myself dog savvy. I always had a special calling to help the shy, timid ones. I've dealt with scared dogs before. I liked seeing them grow emotionally and gain confidence. *I knew I was giving myself a major pep talk.*

"Are you SURE you want her?" Robin emailed.

"I am sure. I want Louise," I emailed back to her.

> ### Beagle Bit
> **Most beagles given up to rescues and shelters are between 7 – 12 months of age, the time when they are most energetic.**

Chapter Three

Be Careful What You Ask For

December 30, 2005, was a brisk, wintry day. Rescue volunteers such as I, who chose a new dog to foster, awaited the arrival of the transport as icy winds breezed through our jackets. Transports are scheduled all over the country on a daily basis to bring animals into rescue, to another shelter, or to their new homes. Furry Friends Network accepts local owner surrenders and strays found in central Pennsylvania. We also foster dogs and cats from animal shelters in our area. But a number of our beagles and hounds, especially unwanted hunting dogs, are transported from high-kill shelters out of state.

There are preassigned destinations for the animals to be brought to certain locations. The route is mapped out and networked on the Internet. Transport coordinators diligently plan each stop's estimated arrival time. Along the journey, fifteen minute potty breaks are built in for the dogs to get out and stretch. Drivers are informed of breeds, weights, medical needs, behavior issues, and correct identifications and descriptions of the dogs in advance. Volunteers sacrifice their time and gas (very appreciated, especially in this day and age) to transfer animals. Each person drives a "leg," which consists of anywhere from an hour to a several hour journey, and delivers the animals to the next driver. Vehicle makes and license plate numbers are established to ensure the safety and security of the animals. Cell phone numbers are provided and the entire trip is monitored by the transport coordinator. After the dogs reach their destinations and are in their foster homes, everyone emails the transport group to let them know how the dogs are adjusting. "He fell fast asleep after his bath and he ate a good supper," or "Who could give up a sweet dog like this?" are usual comments. I am forever indebted to these devoted people who brought my foster dogs to me. Fostering is only one of the many dimensions of rescue. The transporters play a crucial role in saving the dogs' lives. Otherwise, the dogs would have met an early death at the shelter.

In my early days of rescue, I drove a few transports to help out. If I did not have a foster dog, or was in-between getting my foster dogs, I could give up a few hours on a Saturday to drive a leg. On those days, I learned to wear old clothes and bring plenty of paper towels along. Once, I had several puppies that were too young to be crate trained. On top of my car smelling like a baby's soiled diaper, dogs often get carsick on long rides. I sped on the highway with all the car windows rolled down to tolerate the odor. I pulled my shirt over my nose to keep from gagging. It was the longest two-hour drive I ever encountered. Finally arriving at my destination, I handed over the stinky little fur balls to the next person. The puppies squirmed and squawked, eager to be out of the crates. We cleaned the puppies up as best we could, and off they embarked, onto the next "leg." Looking back, I was glad that a few hours of my life played a critical role in theirs.

At the transport site that cold day in December, the soon-to-be fosters, whether for the first time or the "many more" time, made small talk while we stood lingering. Questions filled the air. "Who are you getting today?" "What shelter are they from?" "What kind of dog is it?" "How many foster dogs does that make at your house now?" The transport site also served as a place for the meeting of the minds where fosters caught up on Furry Friends Network news, chit-chatted about family events, or gained moral support from other fosters.

Robin, the head of Furry Friends Network, was also there to hand out our foster kits. This kit consisted of a new collar, leash, dog food, treats, and toys. Robin distributed medications such as de-wormer, flea and tick preventative, and antibiotics for infections such as kennel cough. Supplies are always provided to the foster family by the Furry Friends Network rescue. The foster family pays no out-of-pocket expenses. A foster family gives time, love, and training to a dog. You can't put a price on that.

Finally, the white cargo van pulled in. Everyone exclaimed excitedly, "They're here!" The dogs' seven-hour trip that started in West Virginia was over. One by one, the dogs got out of the van. We *oohed* and *aahed* at cute puppies as they were handed to their fosters. The puppies cuddled against a warm coat sleeve and licked the faces of their new caregivers. Other puppies capered about with elation, freed from the cramped cages. One hound that stepped out was so emaciated it was pitiful. Every rib showed on that dog. His hip bones protruded from each side. I never saw a dog so skinny. I felt sickened.

It was my turn. Tom Renner, a Furry Friends Network volunteer and a good acquaintance, drove the last leg. I peered into the van to search for Louise, scanning the arrangement of crates, piled two and three rows high. This transport van carried almost thirty dogs, stacked like boxes in a warehouse. It was hard to decipher the dogs' appearances through the plastic crate enclosures. Peeking through the metal bars in front, I searched for which dog matched that particular picture of Louise on the Internet, the photo of Louise that I had admired for so long.

"There she is!" I said excitedly as I spotted her.

Tom looked at me and shook his head when I found Louise. He informed me that there had been some trouble with both Thelma and Louise at the last leg. Thelma bit the driver. Both dogs were so scared that they were out of control. "We had to shove them back in their crates. They were hard to handle. They wouldn't let us pick them up," reported Tom. I listened anxiously and wondered what I had gotten myself into. "You got the lesser of the two evils," Tom said to me quietly as I reached for Louise.

With what Tom told me in mind, I had a firm grip on Louise and managed to get her out of the crate. I quickly fastened a leash on her. She bucked and pulled away from me.

At first, I wasn't terribly concerned. In my experience, many beagles that were penned hunting dogs were not comfortable wearing a leash. It was a new and frightening feeling for them. They did not understand what was tugging at their neck, but later grew accustomed to it. Louise was extremely skittish and scuttled all over the place. Even for her small twenty-pound stature, restraining and regulating her movements was difficult. Her actions seemed unnatural, different from normal pent-up energy.

Robin directed me to hold Louise still while she placed a no-slip collar on her. Louise struggled as though we were branding her. A no-slip collar tightens as the animal pulls on it, similar to a choker. We did not want her getting loose. Frightened dogs at previous transports have slipped right out of a regular collar as they writhed and squirmed or if the collar was too big. Your heart sinks to your stomach when a dog wriggles loose and is on the run. A no-slip collar cannot come off and inhibits the dog's ability to escape.

Robin noticed there was something wrong about Louise's mannerisms. She had a worried look on her face. This behavior seemed atypical, even for a rescue dog. Our eyes locked. We each had a feeling that something didn't seem right. Robin probably thought, *You're going to have your hands full.* But she reassured me by saying, "She'll be fine with you, Sharon. Do your 'beagle magic' on her." Her voice sounded uneasy.

"I'll work with her," I replied.

Reeling in Louise by her leash, I picked up her unyielding little body and plopped her in the crate in my car. Rescue dogs always needed a bath, and I couldn't take a chance on poop or throw up ending up on my car seat.

"It'll be all right," I said to Louise on the way home. "That was the last Christmas you'll spend in a hog pen." I talked to her in the car so she would get used to my voice. "Aren't you glad to be out of that shelter?" I said in a gentle voice, trying to comfort her.

I could only imagine what Louise had been through. Rescued dogs encounter drastic changes in a matter of a few short days. Shelters are very stressful places for animals - the echoes of barking and whining dogs they do not know, new smells of strangers both human and dogs, maybe a different food, detachment from their owners, and having people they have never seen before take care of them. Shelter shock sets in if a dog was taken from a warm, cozy home to a cold, concrete kennel. Natural depression and uncertainty manifest themselves. The fortunate ones make it out. Then they endure the transport ride. Most are spayed or neutered before they are released from the facility. I can only imagine the pangs of having a hysterectomy, then traveling for seven hours the following day. Now Louise, already strained, was headed for yet another unfamiliar place. My home.

Louise's newest adventure, and mine, had just begun.

Beagle Bit

In the U.S., beagles are classified into two sizes: 13 and 15 inches, measuring from the top of the shoulders (the withers) to the ground.

Chapter Four

Louise's Newest Adventure

My own beagles greeted me with a chorus of howls at my bay window as I pulled into my snowy driveway. I carried Louise in her crate directly into the house. She plastered herself to the rear of the crate, unwilling to exit. After practically dumping her out of the crate, she was evasive and elusive. Most previous fosters could not wait to leave the crate and catapulted forward as soon as I opened the door. Not Louise.

Hiding in a corner, even after she had been out of her crate for a while, Louise would not be in the same room with Ray and me. She would not walk past us or get near us. Tail wedged between her legs, her body was in a stationary, winced position. Her forehead was permanently wrinkled with worry. When I called her to come to me, she retreated as if I was the enemy. If I reached out to pet her, she averted me. If I got too near, Louise did an emergency take-off away from me. I never saw a dog react that way to me before. Most fosters were happy to be out of the shelter. They exhibited bursts of energy and zoomed through each room in the house exploring. They were hyper in a playful way. They frolicked and acted crazy when they got here, tossing doggy toys in the air or chasing my dogs. A house with lots of scents got their beagle noses sniffing and scouring the rugs. They investigated everything from the kitchen trash can to my smelly sneakers. *Hallelujah,* they thought. *This sure beats the shelter!* But Louise didn't act happy at all. Her body hunched over in cowardice. Ray and I looked at each other in bewilderment.

"This one's going to take some time," I said quietly and looked at Ray.

The next day, my sister, Denise, and her family came over for New Year's Eve. Denise had experience dealing with nervous, scared dogs in her grooming shop. She could help me assess Louise. But the sight of three more people in our home sent Louise in a tizzy. Even though they didn't touch her, she backed up and couldn't get far enough away from them. My 12' x 18' family room wasn't long enough or big enough for Louise. She repelled people of any gender or age. She appeared to be having a panic attack.

Her body thrashed with seizure-like convulsions at the sight of a human. Denise was dumbfounded.

"It's almost as if her brain short circuits," Denise said. "It looks like someone is shocking her." Louise's body was nothing but palsies.

The only way I could respond was creasing up my forehead and saying, "I picked a real doozy, didn't I?"

My family stayed a few more hours to celebrate the incoming New Year. Louise was not celebrating. She withdrew to an upstairs bedroom, the farthest in the house.

Denise left with a "good luck with this one" look on her face. It was getting late. Ray and I went to bed. A few minutes later, I checked on the whereabouts of Louise. She was curled up, sleeping in a pet bed in the living room. *That's the most relaxed I've seen her*, I thought. *Maybe tomorrow will be better.*

With only a few more days of Christmas vacation remaining, I focused on acclimating Louise. I buried myself in books about fearful dogs. Some lines of beagles had an inherent disposition to shyness. A genetically shy beagle will usually remain somewhat introverted. But proper socialization and careful training would help these dogs assuage their timidity. Some suggestions to help a bashful dog are to stoop when you approach it. Standing is threatening to a dog. Avoid direct eye contact. And do not reach overhand to pet a dog. That is considered a dominant move. Pet underhand instead. Let the dog adjust and come to you in its own time. I studied everything from homeopathic medicines to Tellington TTouch Training™ by Linda Tellington-Jones, which is circular massaging, to calm Louise.

Massage Louise? I couldn't even pet her. The first thing I had to do was catch her.

One morning before school I chased her around my dining room table like we were racing laps in the Indy 500 to get her outside to potty. Since she had two more legs than I had, I ran out of gas first. "Come, Louise," was not working. I crouched down and said, "Mum, mum." For some reason unbeknownst to me, Louise stopped dead in her tracks. I have no idea why I said something so silly, but it worked. "Mum, mum" was not listed in any obedience manuals as a command, but I didn't care. Taking advantage of the opportunity, I scooped her up. Her body was frozen in fear. Her muscles were so rigid and tight, I thought she was a piece of steel. And those eyes. She has amber colored eyes. When I picked her up, her brow crunched up like a crinkle-cut french fry. Her pupils got as big as saucers. She had a horrified look on her face, like car lights shining into the eyes of a deer. I gently caressed her, hoping to show her that being held was consoling. She would have none of that.

Luckily, Louise had three traits that were my saving grace. First, she was food motivated. Beagles are generally indiscriminate eaters. I tempted and coaxed her with food. I tossed morsels to lure her and then was able to grab and pick her up. Second, Louise got along well with the other beagles here. She followed their cues. She initially ran from the banging of the garage screen door or the whoosh of the sliding glass door in my dining room. But eventually, she scuffled past them, trailing behind my dogs. These constituted triumphs for Louise. Third, Louise had a curiosity that worked to her advantage. She'd muster up courage and peek at us from another room, hiding around a corner, investigating our activity.

I knew that Louise's issues were not ordinary. Something was very wrong. Louise was far beyond the normal wary dog that I've experienced with my fosters, even in the most severe cases of abuse or neglect. Most fosters were "a piece of cake," settling in my home and bonding with me immediately. Ray had a worse time with introducing himself to Louise. He was disheartened that she ran from him. We resorted to keeping a leash on her in the house so he could take her outside.

Even though I was well-versed in beagles, I needed assistance with managing Louise. I emailed Robin for guidance, "Houston, we have a problem." I explained Louise's shortcomings. Robin referred me to a local certified dog behaviorist, Terri Bullers. It turned out that Thelma's foster mom had already sought recommendations a few days before I asked for help. Terri's take on Thelma and Louise was that they were never socialized at a young age. They had little contact with people. If human bonding is not done in the formative weeks of a developing puppy, seven to twelve weeks being the most critical time, the results can be devastating. The dogs' behavior was similar to feral (wild) cats. Sometimes it can be reversed, but it is a long and slow process. Most unsocialized dogs remain loners and aloof – not your "wag the tail, meet and greet" kind of dog – definitely not the best characteristics for a dog that is up for adoption. There are so many friendlier ones to choose from.

It may not have been what *was* done to Thelma and Louise; it was what *wasn't* done that caused their severe behavior challenges. "The girls," as we called them, were probably stuck in a kennel and the key thrown away, so to speak. Terri instructed me to show Louise that the world was a good and safe place. Be positive and upbeat. Use treats to motivate her. No babying her; that will only reinforce her scared behavior.

It was hard for me to block my maternal instincts and not coddle Louise. Seeing her so scared, my first reaction was to pamper her. *Poor baby, you've had an awful life,* I thought. I wanted to rock her and cradle her in my arms. I suppressed my desire to sing lullabies. I admit I had empty nest syndrome. My own daughters were grown and out of the house. But in training a dog, you cannot reward undesirable behavior. I put a big smile on my face as I held Louise. I told her, "You are such a brave girl," in a happy, confident way.

When I'd pass Louise in the house going about my daily business, I'd say, "Hi, Louise. How ya' doin'?" in a happy-go-lucky way. I didn't look at her. I didn't try to pet her. Just being in the same room with me was an advancement for Louise. Louise studied me. Little by little, she crept closer. She realized that I, perhaps the first real caregiver in her life, was not someone to fear.

Louise's rehabilitation was essential to her becoming adopted. School was back in session after the holiday break, but I was determined to help her all I could. I read several of Cesar Millan's books, including *Cesar's Way, Cesar's Rules,* and *Cesar's Short Guide to a Happy Dog* (I suppose for Louise, Cesar may have to write another version of that book, *"Long" Guide to a Happy Dog!*). Cesar, known as The Dog Whisperer, writes of three universal components to owning a well-adjusted canine: exercise, firm leadership and discipline, and love – in that order.[2] Most people make the mistake of putting affection first. We all love our dogs, but this humanizes them. We forget a dog is a dog. I wasn't supposed to woo and coo Louise. Terri had advised me to not coddle Louise or baby her. Next, dogs need guidance and structure. They look up to their owner to be their pack leader. Louise needed my steadfast direction to overcome her obstacles. Foremost is exercise. Because many people work full time, it is common for a

---

2 Cesar Millan, *Cesar's Way, The Natural Everyday Guide to Understanding & Correcting Common Dog Problems,* page 198-199.

dog to be crated for an eight-hour workday. Hence, anxiety and boredom can set in. The dog can become overly rambunctious or destructive. Daily walking is essential, even for dogs that have a fenced yard. The walk is a time for you to bond with your dog.

My recipe for fostering had always been taking lots of walks. I managed to take several walks a day, even while teaching a full day. Beagles love walks, too. They are working dogs. They love to sniff, dragging their noses to the ground. That's what they were bred to do. It was ingrained in their genetics. I tired my dogs out so much by walking that they had little interest in destroying anything in my house.

That's it! That was my new philosophy for Louise's therapy plan. Louise must learn to be a beagle on the walk, and not scrambling all over like a confused squirrel. She didn't even know she was a dog. After I was able to get my hands on Louise, the next step in her rehabilitation was the walk. That would make her normal, or so I hoped.

Louise was a mess on our walks. She had jerky gyrations because of not comprehending the feel of the leash. This was compounded by her abhorrent fear of people and noises. Her erratic behavior was a prescription for disaster. We awoke at 6:00 a.m. I made my coffee and fed the dogs. Walks started around 6:45 a.m. We'd walk an hour before I had to leave for school. My strategy was that I took Louise on her walks that early so she could see people getting in their cars and leaving for work. She kept her distance from them. If anyone came within twenty feet of her, she went into a "fight or flight" mode. I called it her "terror mode." Not only did we have to deal with people, noises also set off an alarm in her brain. Her daunting reaction to car doors slamming and a school bus's diesel engine *va-r-r-r-ooming* by indicated she had previously had little exposure to the outside world.

In spite of the difficulties, I carried out my plan. We braved the frigid January weather. I bundled up in my heavy, purple, down coat, wrapped my scarf around my face with only my eyeballs showing, and wore my thermal-lined gloves. I trudged onward, beagles in tow. In the cold, bitter evenings, I wore a reflective blinker as we have no streetlights where I live in the country. Sometimes in the dark, I could hear the howls of coyotes in our nearby mountain and I got as scared as Louise.

One morning on the walk, I spotted the rounded roof of the garbage truck appearing over the hill. *Oh no,* I thought. *Louise is going to freak!* I could hear the screech of the hydraulic lift as it stopped to pick up trash. There was nowhere to turn. We were surrounded by woods. The green monster was coming our way! As we approached the uproar, Louise bolted away from the clamor. Luckily, the no-slip collar did its job and prevented her from squirming away. I didn't like seeing it tighten around her neck, but it kept her from fleeing. We made it past the voluminous vehicle. *Whew, we got by that one,* I thought.

If Louise ever did get loose, that would be an unthinkable disaster; I shuddered to even have that thought enter my mind.

Other than dealing with Louise, I enjoyed walking my beagles. It provided exercise and mental therapy for me, too. I'd rehearse my lessons in my head and think of my "to do" list on the morning walk. *I'll have the kids write examples of improper fractions on their whiteboards,* I thought. *I must remember to send Jonathan's work home while he is out sick. I need to ask the other third grade teacher to exchange recess duty with me.* Afternoon walks allowed me to reflect on the day's activities, assess my lessons, and wind down. *I should have used fraction flashcards for the children who needed more practice*, I thought. *Boy, Paul was sure full of himself today. How can I better manage him tomorrow?*

My neighbors would often see me pass by their houses two or three times a day. They'd holler, "Didn't you walk those dogs by here already today? No wonder you're so thin."

"Keeps me fit and trim," I always replied with a smile.

One day while walking our old beagle-mix dog, Nellie, my neighbor, Steve Reightler, stopped working in his yard to thank me for some dog treats I'd given him. He started to cross the street to come over to us. "Please stay on your side," I warned him. "This little dog is very scared of people." He went back over by his house as I stood across the road. We spoke briefly for a minute or two.

I glanced down at Louise and she was gone! All I saw was half of a frazzled leash dangling in mid-air. I was so surprised it took me a minute to realize what had happened. Louise gnawed through the leash like a beaver would have gnawed through a matchstick. "How'd she chew through that? How'd she get away so fast without me noticing?" I yelled over to my neighbor. I panicked.

Steve offered to hold the leash with my senior dog, Nellie. Nellie's delicate state of health and frail body couldn't dash up the hill with me to find Louise. I sprinted like a marathon runner. I spotted Louise in my next-door neighbor's yard. I ran into my house, grabbed hot dogs, and pitched them at her. The food hound that she was, the hot dogs thankfully attracted Louise. I shoveled her into my arms. We got inside, my neighbor returned Nellie, and I took a deep breath that Louise was back home safe.

That night I showed Ray the gnashed leash. He couldn't believe his eyes. "She's going to drive us to drink," he said, only half-kidding.

Once again, it crossed my mind, and just as quickly I pushed that thought as far away as I could, *If Louise ever did get loose outside the neighborhood, she is so scared, we'd never find her.*

Despite her enormous faults, Robin and Terri felt that Louise would eventually improve and surmount her fears. To my advantage, Louise never showed any aggression. Other than being scared, she was a likable little dog. Robin and Terri felt with time, Louise would fit into the right household. Because she was a foster dog, Louise was advertised on our Furry Friends Network website. I carefully wrote a description of her, hoping to attract a very special applicant who'd want a special needs dog. It went something like this: *I am a twenty-pound red and white copper- nosed beagle who needs a permanent, loving home. I am very scared right now. I will need a low-key, quiet home. It may take me a while to warm up to you, so please be patient with me.*

An applicant who previously applied to Furry Friends Network for another beagle wanted to meet Louise. To be fair, I leveled with her. I kept no secrets about Louise's flaws, but this person was still interested. The family was exactly the kind of people I wanted for Louise. Louise would only be alone a few hours a day because of their flexible working schedules. They had a son in college and no young, active children that may frighten or mishandle her. They formerly owned a beagle and were experienced with the breed. They seemed sincere and compassionate.

As a next step, I took Louise to their house for a short visit. She was frightened and cowered, but the wife, Marge, connected with her. While I held Louise's stiff body,

Marge petted her. Marge's soft-spoken and gentle demeanor did not frighten Louise. At one point, Louise jumped on the couch and Marge was able to sit a few feet from her.

"I'm already seeing progress in her," I said to Marge. "Let's take things slowly and I'll bring her to your home to visit a few more times."

Several succinct visits followed. I hoped to ease Louise's transition to a new home. I stayed an hour or two while Louise mostly paced. I explained how they could best manage her behavior, cope with her shyness, and continue her training. Marge was still willing to give it a try. She thought Louise was cute and also probably pitied her. They had empty hearts because their beagle had died recently. Louise would fill that void. They also owned a nine-year-old Dalmatian who Louise took a liking to. At these visits, I stayed, and for the most part, Louise did as well as could be expected.

Then, we upped the ante and decided to let Louise stay overnight with them. I dropped Louise off on a Friday evening. We made arrangements for me to pick her up Saturday at 4:00 p.m. That night, I could hardly sleep and wondered how Louise was doing. Every time the phone rang on Saturday morning, I thought it was Marge. My gut feeling was right. Saturday at 1:00 p.m., a frustrated voice on the line said, "You can come to get her now."

"Did something happen? Is she all right?" I questioned.

Marge told me they had taken Louise out late at night to potty and could not get her back inside. She wouldn't budge. As soon as they reached for her, they saw Louise's true colors. They never saw a dog that scared. This wasn't the kind of dog they wanted to adopt. When most people are grieving after losing a pet, they want the new dog to reciprocate their affection. Then on Saturday morning, Louise went into terror mode. A neighbor got too near when Marge took her out to potty. Even their neighbor commented, "She's a piece of work."

Later, they made the mistake of taking off Louise's leash in the house. Of course, they could not catch her. Louise wanted nothing to do with the husband or son. They were now sure that this was not a good match. I can't say I blamed them. When I retrieved Louise, I thanked them for their interest in Louise and apologized for any inconvenience. I drove home thinking it's only been a few weeks since I had Louise and she needed more time in foster care. Whatever was or wasn't done to this dog wasn't her fault.

When I got home, I emailed Robin and Terri, suggesting Louise be taken off our website. I considered her unadoptable at this point. She simply could not adjust to new surroundings yet. She could not be re-homed without complications. Louise had profound issues. Her behavior was more than the average pet owner was equipped to handle. Besides, who would pay a several hundred-dollar adoption fee for a dog they could not pet? I couldn't bear to place Louise in a new environment when she could hardly function in mine. Louise was not ready for the world.

Perhaps the world was not ready for Louise.

Beagle Bit

Your beagle may do "reverse sneezing." This is characterized by rapid and repeated forced inhalation through the nose, accompanied by snorting or gagging sounds. It sounds like the dog is choking. An episode may last one – two minutes. It is not harmful, and occurs when the soft palate and throat become irritated.

Chapter Five

Good-bye to Our Nel Nel

Instead of embracing my role as Louise's rescuer, I regretted it. The timing was bad. This was the worst time to have chosen a foster dog as needy as Louise. I was in it for the long haul; that was my commitment. Most of my fosters got adopted quickly, but this would not be the case with Louise. My big, soft heart got me into a big, hard predicament. My devotion should have been directed toward Nellie, our fifteen-year-old beagle-mix, who was in her dying days. Instead, I doted on Louise, sinking hours into daily walks and researching strategies on dealing with fearful dogs in hopes of transforming her. I felt guilty at times for emotionally neglecting Nellie. Louise's rehabilitation spread me so thin I barely had time for Nellie's geriatric care.

Over Christmas vacation, a few days before Louise first made her appearance at our home, I had taken Nellie to get chest x-rays. Her outlook was grim. If the lung tumor burst or was near her heart, she'd go fast. The vet told us to take her home and let her finish living the rest of her days.

Oddly, when Louise arrived, she was the only foster dog that Nellie would let interact with her, even on her worst days. Louise loved to snuggle and lay on the couch almost on top of Nellie. I suspected Louise had been used to hovering with her sister, Thelma, most of her life. Since Nellie was aged when I began fostering, she never played with any of the foster beagles and preferred to be left alone. She was twelve years old when Riley, contrary and headstrong, came into the picture. Nellie didn't want anything to do with him. He pestered her. But Nellie accepted Louise and they formed an unlikely bond.

Long before my Furry Friends Network days and my involvement in rescue, we found Nellie in a newspaper ad. We paid a whopping thirty-five dollars for her and played a trick on our two daughters when we had arranged to pick her up and bring her to our home.

Our daughters, Alicia and Jessica, were in elementary school at the time. They were at the neighbor's house playing with their friends when it was time to leave to get

Nellie. We told them Ray was purchasing a tool from an ad and they had to go along with us. They fussed and questioned us about our reasoning but we insisted on taking them. They had no interest in a tool, and besides, the neighbor invited them to stay and continue playing. In our, *"You better listen if you know what's good for you"* parent tone of voice, we demanded they come along. The girls balked at accompanying us. They were sourpusses in the car during the whole trip there.

When we arrived at our destination, nine eight-week-old yippy, yappy beagle-basset puppies, ears dragging and hind ends wiggling, ran out to meet the girls. "Look, they have puppies here," exclaimed Alicia, running towards them. Ray and I looked at each other; they still didn't get it. The joke was on them.

"Surprise, pick one!" Ray and I cried out. "We're not here to buy a tool, we're here to get a puppy!"

When they realized we had fooled them, the girls had looks on their faces like, *"Good one, Mom and Dad!"*

One particular puppy, of the nine, ran to Alicia and immediately licked her face and cuddled with her. It seems like Nellie picked us to be a part of our family. Ray named her by thinking of "Whoa, Nellie" because of her rambunctious puppy playfulness. So, that is how Nellie got her name.

The drive home was quite a contrast to the drive there. Two little girls could not have been happier. Frowns transformed into broad smiles that were implanted on their faces from ear to ear. Their braces gleamed like the sun reflecting on a mirror on a clear, sunny day. Of course, Nellie "christened" Alicia by peeing on her lap. Alicia didn't care one bit. She now had a puppy.

For fifteen years, Nellie was a member of our family. She saw me encounter major surgeries, our move from a townhouse in the suburbs to a sprawling home in the country, to the girls' graduations, to Alicia's wedding, Jessica's move to Florida, and through many other family milestones. Nellie was a hit with everyone she met. "Look at her big, velvety-brown ears!" people would comment. But more important than Nellie's soft ears, was Nellie's great disposition. We raised her from a puppy so she had no emotional baggage like many of the fosters. She was that great family dog that everyone would want to have. Our very own Lassie. Well, almost. She would never be as obedient as the famed collie. Beagles can be "rock heads." My husband, Ray, teased us that he was outnumbered by yet another stubborn female in the house.

Back to the present, while Nellie snoozed with labored breathing lying next to me, I recollected her longevity with us. Her heavy breaths whisked my skin. Louise came and cuddled with us. We three girls made a tight trio. Thinking of the past fifteen years, I recalled some of Nellie's mishaps. She had some close calls where she almost didn't survive until this ripe, old age. We often quipped that she had nine lives, like they say about cats.

Memories flooded into my mind, the time over the years seemed to go so fast; the time was coming soon for her to leave us. One time Nellie sneaked into my daughter, Jessica's, bedroom, where an opened box of chocolate-covered cookies awaited our curious beagle. Nellie gobbled down the entire box. Now, we all have a sweet tooth here at the Cree household, but chocolate is lethal to dogs because it contains a substance called theobromine. I made an urgent call to the vet. Luckily, dark baking chocolate poses more risk. He told us to watch for symptoms such as lethargy or vomiting. We kept a close eye on Nellie all evening, certain she'd puke or worse, keel over. But nothing like that happened and by the next morning, Nellie was frolicking and romping around the yard. She somehow dodged that bullet. And as a result, she didn't learn her lesson.

Nellie and Louise are both notorious chow hounds. Once Louise snatched a blueberry muffin from me and ate it, paper and all. Like Louise, Nellie thought that any food left lying around was fair game. One time Jessica made herself a bologna and cheese sandwich. She stepped aside to answer the phone, leaving it unattended. Upon returning to what should have been her lunch, the plate sat empty. The sandwich magically disappeared. Nellie looked at Jessica with her innocent, droopy brown eyes. She happily licked her chops with evidence of a mustard mustache as if to say, "Got sandwich?"

Nellie also had an inkling toward inedible substances. One day when I came home midday to put Louise out to potty, while Louise preferred to eat tissues out of the trash can, Nellie had more fun taking the toilet paper and running with it – all through the house! Streamers of shredded toilet tissue were strewn down the steps like a ticker tape parade.

The list of Nellie experiences continued, lined up like a row of soldiers marching through my mind, one by one. There was the time I was sick with a sinus infection and found the old-fashioned glass thermometer that was next to my bed on the floor in a million slithers, mercury dancing on the floor, almost impossible to pick up. Nellie must have mistaken it for a rawhide stick. Luckily, Nellie had no sign of glass shards in her mouth or poisonous mercury that she could have ingested. Once again, she dodged death; her body temperature remained normal.

And then, there's the time that she dragged her body along the floor, crawling on her belly as if in combat dodging enemy gunfire, howling in excruciating pain. We didn't know what she ate, or what was causing the extreme discomfort. The girls bawled, assuming she was on her deathbed. We all made a quick trip to the vet in Ray's truck, the girls and Nellie cuddled together in our makeshift ambulance. Turned out Miss Bone Head ate so much grass after we mowed the lawn, she had gas. Poor baby! Nothing a good dose of gas medicine wouldn't remedy. I laughed out loud at this memory, so long ago, and yet, it seemed just like yesterday.

The stories kept coming to mind, and with them, a smile: my pair of brand new sixty-dollar leather heels seemed to magically display teeth marks on them as if they were a new dog toy, and the time I wrapped Christmas packages early and put them under the tree, where they remained untouched, until three days before Christmas, when our whole family went out to finish our gift shopping. When we returned from the mall, exhausted from dealing with other last-minute shoppers like us, all the packages were opened, bows, boxes and contents strewn everywhere…but, not one gift was harmed! How did Nellie know not to shred the gifts? Then there was the time when she got a bee sting on her ear and it swelled to the size of an elephant's. Nellie could have been the poster child for antihistamine medicine.

And, one story that could be a book in itself…when Nellie played with a wax ring from the toilet that Ray was working on, smearing a thick oozing gel-like substance all over our carpets. It took a professional carpet cleaning service to get it out. Ray was so angry his ears were red…Nellie, on the other hand, had no idea what she did wrong!

And, in the process, Nellie ingested a screw…which later came out of her. Ray shook his head and said, seriously, "Nellie's got a screw loose!"

So many more memories raced through my mind, all very special for the special dog that Nellie was in our lives. That's what people do when their dog is dying. You remember the good old days. You mourn the good with the bad. You recall all those times you were so angry at your dog and you laugh about them now when it is time to cry. You reminisce about its quirks. You forgive it because you love it. And, you pray that you could just have one more chance where your dog gets on your very last nerve.

Nellie's body functions were failing her. She hadn't eaten or drank in days. The vet suggested I buy meat baby food, but Nellie refused it. Her eyelids sagged. Her hearing weakened. She became disoriented while out in the yard although she could still physically get up and around. Her nine lives were up. Her condition worsened.

On Friday, January 27, 2006, the day preceding his birthday, Ray left for work in the early dawn hours. I did some quick chores around the house before school and walked the dogs. I had been diligently working with Louise, and by now, she welcomed the walks. Although still afraid of people, she got excited at seeing the leash and knew the words, "Go for a walk?" But Nellie could not go for a walk with us that morning. Although she could walk, she was too sick to exercise. She stood at the door with a gaunt look on her face as if asking, "Why can't I come along?"

At school, I received a call from Ray. I was stunned because he rarely phoned me at work. In all the years we were married, I could count the calls on one hand where he interrupted the office secretary. I knew it was urgent. The news, though foreseeable, was unexpected. He made an appointment to have Nellie euthanized at 3:30 p.m. that day. Then it hit me. Nellie was going to die today.

I was almost relieved Ray made the appointment. Nellie would not have to suffer any more. The sleepless nights took a toll on me as well. Three cups of coffee fueled my day. With Nellie at the age of fifteen, I knew this day was inevitable. I found comfort that, unlike rescue dogs, Nellie never went hungry. She was never mistreated or homeless. We could only conjecture Louise's history of abuse and neglect, but Nellie had a good life. We treated her like a queen.

We got to the vet's just in time. When picking Nellie up to take her out of the car, the tumor must have ruptured. I carried Nellie's semi-lifeless body into the waiting room. The receptionist saw the look on my face and said, "Take her right back, Sharon."

"She was a lucky dog and lived a good life. She had *you*," our vet told us. Holding Nellie's paw, we stayed in the room throughout the euthanasia procedure. I never saw Ray cry before in our seventeen-year marriage, even at his father's funeral. But, he shed tears over Nellie.

When we got home, Ray insisted on digging Nellie's grave immediately. We chose a spot in our backyard bordering the woods at the base of the mountain. Nellie liked to explore and sniff there, putting her hound dog skills to work. Actually, another Nellie trait, she'd dilly-dally in the yard and came when she felt like listening. Ray, of course, emotionally distraught, was also not feeling well physically. He'd recently recovered from a bad bout of bronchitis and had a slight fever. The ground was hard and frozen in the dead of winter. "It has to be done now," he said. Ray dug like a madman, sweating profusely. This was his tribute to Nellie and her memory.

We did not celebrate Ray's birthday the following day. Other years, I enjoyed having a big family gathering. I liked fussing, making a spread of food, and hosting company. But that year was different. No one felt like rejoicing the birth of a life, when another life so special was just taken from us.

Ray and I coped with Nellie's death in our separate ways. With Louise at my side, I sat on the back porch, with the peace and solace of my wooded back yard. I dipped a chocolate covered cookie in my coffee, saying, "This one's for you, Nellie." While I put Nellie's photos around the house for every visitor to see, assigned my class to write a story about their pet's antics, placed flowers and arranged garden stones around her grave, Ray grieved in a different way. Ray is a reserved man; he's a "mean what you say and say what you mean" kind of guy. Once you get to know him, you discover his sense of humor. Ray was quieter than his normal self, said very little, moped and was forlorn. He had no interest in doing any of his manly chores around the house, even if I reminded him politely. He pretended to read his evening paper, but I saw his eyes drift off the page and his mind wandered. We did not have our ordinary conversations at the supper table where he asked, "What happened in school today? Did the kids drive you crazy?" I attempted to cheer him up by telling witty scenarios of my teaching day, only getting a one or two word response. He grieved privately.

All Ray murmured in the weeks to come was, "I miss my Nel Nel."

Beagle Bit

Beagles currently hold the №5 position on AKC "America's 10 Most Popular Dog Breed List." The beagle is the only breed to rank in the top ten every year since their AKC registry.

Chapter Six

Relentless Rehabilitation

    Why in the world did Louise enter my life? This I pondered constantly. Was she some kind of cosmic plan in the grand scheme of my life? Were our paths destined to cross because I had the patience to deal with her phobias? Would I have the power within me to convert this neurotic dog into a terrific pet for some family? Was she sent to replace Nellie? And, sometimes, I just wondered if Louise was sent into my life to drive me crazy! There were no answers, just questions.

Ray and I continued to experience sorrow over the loss of our beloved beagle-mix Nellie in our own personal and distinct styles. Ray puttered about the house in his placid mode seeming lost in life. He felt an emptiness, a hollowness that wretches the heart. I accepted Nellie's death and celebrated the fifteen years she shared with us. But, seeing her empty food dish and unused leash still saddened me greatly. We still had our two other beagles, Riley and BuddyLee. They filled the house with unremitting dog hair, barking, muddy paw prints, and companionship. And suffice it to say, caring for Louise deluged me.

Louise's rehabilitation constantly overwhelmed me. It had now been one month since Louise arrived at our home. Shortly before Nellie died, our daughter Jessica came to visit from Florida where she lived and worked. Our daughter was all grown up and had moved out of state for her job. It made me feel good that she got to see Nellie one last time. However, with Jessica visiting, Louise acted like she was afraid of her own shadow. She would not stay in the same room with Jessica. Jessica had told her friend about this psycho little dog her mom was fostering. "Wait'll you see this weirdo," she said to her friend on the phone.

"Send me a picture of her," he replied. Jessica positioned her cell phone and snapped a picture of Louise. When her friend received the picture, he texted back, "Where's Louise? I thought you sent me her picture." Louise vanished so quickly upon seeing Jessica that the picture was of an empty room. Rare moments like this made me laugh, but I cried inside.

When Jessica returned back to her home in Florida, she told me, "That dog's sure not a Nellie." And, she was right, of course. Louise was not like any other dog.

Remembering that Nellie wanted to go for a walk even on her last dying day, I listened to my gut feeling and put credence in Cesar Millan, The Dog Whisperer's advice. Exercise was the key to unlocking Louise's make up. Not only did I talk the talk, but I walked the walk, literally. Louise became excited at the rattle of the leash. She wagged her tail and shimmied her torso, eagerly anticipating the outings. Walk, walk, walk. Day in and day out. With Riley and BuddyLee as her mentors, I walked Louise so much I thought my feet were going to fall off. Even my furry, black snow boots gave me blisters. My fingertips stung from the cold temperatures through my itchy, wool mittens. Braving biting winds, icicles dripped from my nostrils. My frostbitten toes thawed by the crackling warmth of my fireplace once we got back home. Louise didn't mind the cold weather one bit.

Since dogs investigate primarily from their sense of smell, Louise's olfactory system was in overdrive. The hound in her emerged as she acquainted herself with the smells of the country, white tail erect, nosing and zigzagging to capture a scent. Louise lunged forward pulling as though she was hauling a load of watermelons. She scraped that twitching copper nose along the hibernating frozen grass. No more scurrying wildly about like she was dodging land mines. Louise was a beagle and she meant business! She barked and bayed at what was unapparent and invisible to me in the snow but caught her instincts. As long as she did not notice any people or hear a loud noise, she would act like a normal dog. The canine in her peaked; I knew it! I knew I would eventually bring the beagle out in Louise! One barrier between Louise and the world slowly started to crumple. The walks were the venue for Louise's transformation. We were making progress.

Although Louise was showing improvement on the walks, her rehabilitation involved many other aspects. She had several other issues that needed to be addressed before she could be adopted. Louise was still a bundle of nerves, and because of that, she peed and pooped as much, and as often, as a puppy. Louise was estimated to be between one and two years of age. But she squatted on my rugs and urinated every hour. If that wasn't bad enough, Louise had nervous defecation, which means with her mental state, she pooped many times per day. You know the saying, "It scared the crap out of me." That was an understatement for Louise.

Most people thought there was an easy solution to her potty problems. Crate her. Easier said than done. We are talking about Louise. Louise hated the crate, whereas most dogs consider it their comfy den. She went bonkers at being confined, not able to pace away her anxiety and if frightened, had nowhere to run. She wanted out like a caged lion. She chewed the plastic latch to an unrecognizable mold of jagged edges. She gnashed the metal bars. One day as I held Louise, her teeth were silver. *No, dogs don't have braces,* I thought. It looked like she had a mouthful of fillings. Chrome slivers appeared to be glued in the enamel of her teeth. Miss Metal Mouth did a real number on her crate…and, her teeth. And she still had accidents in it. Every day when I arrived home from school, outside in the cold of winter, I scrubbed and hosed down the stinky, smelly mess she had made in her crate.

People couldn't understand why I crated Louise when we had installed a pet door for our dogs. You'd think with a pet door it would be easy to housetrain Louise. *No, siree!* That was of no use to Louise. She wouldn't get near it. She wanted nothing to do with it. The slapping sound of the plastic door scared her into next month. The winter weather was too cold for me to prop open the flap, letting out all our home's heat. Many fosters learned the pet door in a jiffy, sometimes the first day they arrived. They'd just follow my dogs out. I tried desperately for weeks to teach Louise to use the pet door, holding it open and coaxing her with treats, gently pushing her through it, but to no avail. She couldn't equate using it to going out to potty. Louise's disturbed little brain couldn't put two and two together.

There were times with housetraining Louise that I felt like *I* needed rescued. I felt chagrin and defeated with Louise. Beagles are generally hard to housetrain. They can be obstinate and bullheaded. However, even when my foster beagles had previously lived a life outside in a pen, I had little trouble getting them house broken. I took them out often, walked them, and rewarded them for appropriate behavior. A potential adopter usually asked as a first question, "Is the dog housetrained?" I worked hard to accomplish that.

Louise was an entirely different story. Louise suffered from submissive urination, which meant she'd eliminate to show submission. This is not to be confused with excitement urination. A subservient dog will display cowering, flattened ears, and its tail tucked under its legs. It boils down to the pack mentality. This is the coy dog's way of showing the pack leader that he (the pack leader) is indeed, the dominant one. This condition occurs in dogs that are insecure, lack confidence, are timid, oversensitive, or intimidated. It is uncontrollable and even dogs that are considered housetrained will submissively urinate. It is not deliberate or spiteful behavior. It happens when owners arrive home, guests enter the house, loud noises or voices are present - anything that scares the dog. It is more prevalent in abused and unsocialized dogs. A mistreated dog constantly feels the need to apologize and show social appeasement. The old method of "sticking the dog's nose in it and giving him a good swat" only makes matters worse. Hence, the scolding makes him even more demure. The dog may pee a bigger puddle. In his mind he's saying, *Look at this big pool of liquid I produced for you. I submitted to you.* In layman's terms, "I was so scared I peed my pants."

Once I understood this concept, I could not become angry at Louise for soiling my carpets. I tenaciously took her out often to housetrain her. I praised her like I was tickled pink that she would potty outside. "Good girl, way to go!" I exclaimed. I was ecstatic for her job well done. Since I couldn't crate Louise and she refused to use the pet door, I came home from school at lunchtime to let her out to potty. This became a daily habit of dropping off my class in the cafeteria, rushing home in the thirty minutes allotted time, and wolfing down a pack of crackers in the car for my midday meal. Even though the school was close to my home, I drove back to school like a maniac, flooring the gas pedal, rushing against the clock. I couldn't be late picking up my students as another boisterous class waited to enter the lunch line. The cafeteria aides gave me angry stares if I was tardy. Because I hadn't eaten enough at noontime, I often became lightheaded and hungry by the afternoons. Honestly, the sacrifices I made for Louise. Ever so slowly Louise's potty accidents in the house lessened, although she still eliminated a copious amount of times for her adult age.

With her housetraining somewhat successful, the mitigating factor in her adoptability remained her fear of people. If I could get that under control, she may not submissively urinate as much. Louise's fear of people infiltrated her entire existence. A kind word or pat on the head would not undo her level of duress. If someone got within close proximity, her eyes filled with a terror that invaded her body and spirit. She looked like she'd seen the Boogeyman and had a meltdown to get away. The crinkled look on her face, the panting, whining, and pacing at the sight of a human indicated an unbalanced emotional state. In rescue we strive to accomplish the three "Rs" – rescue, rehabilitation, and re-home. Louise's reception to any human being, her own three "Rs," were reject, refuse, and retreat.

Did Louise perhaps have a trigger, a particular type of individual that frightened her more so than others? I attempted to discover if there was one. Thinking that height might be the culprit, I observed if toddlers or babies made a difference. Miniature mortals were still two legged. She displayed the same conditioned response of mind-boggling fear to all humans, no matter what age, height or gender.

To better acquaint her to humans, I asked parents and students in my classroom to stop by my house to socialize one of my rescue dogs. The kids jumped at the chance. "You mean I get to see where you live, Mrs. Cree?" they asked. The students rejoiced at the opportunity to help their teacher. As soon as they entered my front door, their excitement turned dismal. *More strangers*, thought Louise. The child crouched down and enticed Louise with treats. Nope, not happenin'. Fear gripped Louise. She only ate the treat if it was tossed within her comfort zone, which was still at least ten feet away. I tried everyone from men with or without beards, men with or without hats, women and men who were built small, nonsmokers, lanky teenagers, little old grannies and grumpy old men. Louise had some sort of post-traumatic stress disorder. It could have been termed – People Traumatic Stress Disorder. If a member of the Homo sapiens species approached Louise, she'd skitter away.

Entertaining company at my house became a dreaded task. I felt like I subjected Louise to cruel and unusual punishment. Her amber snake eyes lit up when guests spilled in. Louise kept her eyes focused, scrutinizing their every move, ready to flee if they came within her vicinity. "Why won't she come to us?" "It looks like she's getting an electric shock when she sees us," were some of the comments my visitors told me. "What's wrong with her?" they asked as they dropped their mouths in disbelief. They were baffled by her uncommon tendencies towards humans. Guests were scary intruders to Louise. She was mortified at their presence. Fear permeated her personality. I hated seeing her repercussions.

Although taken back at first, most people were fascinated by Louise's anthropophobia, fear of people. People would react to her reaction. They gawked at her. Their stunned faces mirrored Louise's frightfulness. "I've never seen a dog so scared," they admitted. "What on earth did someone do to her?" I explained our theory on Louise's upbringing and that she had little to no interaction with people. They felt sorry for her and empathized with what kind of life this poor dog had. "What's wrong with people? They ought to be punished," my guests affirmed. Most people left my house feeling sorry for me, too, thinking, *What are you going to do with this one, Mrs. Cree?* But I was known as a patient and benevolent individual. They knew Louise was at the right place. Little did they know sometimes my patience could turn to fury…and, not at Louise.

Some days I became enraged at the atrocities that must have been done to this little dog. I often thought if I ever met up with Thelma and Louise's original owners, in this life or the next, I'd strangle them with my bare hands. I wanted to wrap my fingers around their scrawny necks and shake the livin' daylights out of them while screaming, "What did you do to this little girl? Look at her. She's a mess! How am I supposed to fix this? How am I going to give her a good life?" I was left to pick up the pieces. Still, I was determined to give Louise the best quality life possible…and successfully find her a forever home.

What was happening to me is what typically happens when you foster. You are very sensitive and emotional in the beginning, then you toughen up, you almost become desensitized to what people have done. Then you get MAD! Then you get over it and work with the rescue dog, concentrating on fixing the dog and not being absorbed in its past.

My outrage at her original owners ignited my passion to work harder to rehabilitate Louise. My anger propelled me and gave me strength. Not only did I feel the anguish that drove me to repair Louise's faults, I felt that she was sent my way for a reason. Maybe the reason was to compensate for the loss of Nellie, and I ran with it.

"Use that magic 'beagle touch' you have, Sharon," Robin at Furry Friends Network told me. I was blessed with a knack for turning around workable behavior problems in my foster dogs. Housetraining, leeriness, and rebuilding trust were issues I addressed with many of the fosters. Now, I wanted to unfold the mysteries of Louise's damaged little mind.

It seemed like I would need to cast a magic spell on Louise to rehabilitate her.

> ## Beagle Bit
>
> Tri-color (black, brown, and white) is the most common fur marking of beagles. Beagles that have a solid black back are called "black blanketed." Some lose their black coloring.

Chapter Seven

Rehabilitation Reinforcement

Louise and I developed some sort of mental telepathy with each other. A nonverbal bond evolved. I was the one person she trusted…the only person she ever trusted.

There were still times we played cat and mouse around the dining room table, but I was usually able to catch her. With other people, she ran for her life. But with me, she stopped and became immobile. Maybe that was her way of telling me, *"Hey, you're not so bad. But, please don't hurt me."* I held and petted her when no one else could, not even Ray. Maybe I was the chosen one. Louise's fate was in my hands.

At times I felt like it was Louise and me against the world. Terri, our Furry Friends Network dog trainer, continued to support me and give me instructions, but I carried them out alone. Normally, a trainer recommends taking the dog to obedience school to establish "leader of the pack." When a dog is successful at commands, the praising and rewards boost its confidence. Louise could not be taken to a public place with all those people. That was not an option. I was her only consort.

If Louise and I could live on a desert island, life would have been peachy. But that was not the case. My goal, and job, was to prepare Louise for being adopted and a chance at her forever home. Beagles are generally not "one person" dogs. They are pack oriented. They love everyone. Everything about Louise went against the grain of her breed. Remembering that Terri suggested to take things gradually, I needed to rehabilitate Louise one person at a time. She trusted me now. Maybe I could expand her horizon by introducing another new person, the same person repeatedly, in a nonthreatening manner.

For this job, I enlisted the help of Barb, the night custodian at my school. I often returned to my classroom in the evening. Since I lived in the same neighborhood, it was not a long distance to travel. It was easier to get work done when I wasn't being interrupted by bells ringing or students calling out, "I'm done, Mrs. Cree. What'll I do next?" Those few hours of quiet and stillness were my sanity time. I usually took a foster dog back into school, where it probed my spacious room and sniffed until its heart's content.

Barb knew me well. She welcomed my visits with all my new four-legged friends when I brought them to the school in the late afternoons and evenings, one at a time. She worked the shift from 3:30 p.m. until midnight. The school was vacant of robust elementary-aged children hurrying out to recess, the teachers' voices sounding out directions, and the principal booming announcements over the loudspeaker. We provided company to her lonely job. All that could be heard was the tinkling sound of the vacuum cleaner sucking up paper clips or toilets flushing and water swirling as she scrubbed them. Then she'd hear the tap, tap, tap of a dog's nails clicking on the glossy tile.

"There's Mrs. Cree with another dog," Barb echoed down the dimly lit hallways. "Who do you have now? What's its story? Can I pet it?" she asked. I told her that particular dog's sad history of abuse, abandonment, or if it narrowly escaped death from a high-kill shelter because of me, and others like me with other rescue dogs, saving it. The foster dog then usually pulled me, ran with excitement, and slid on the shiny, waxed floors, into the custodian's open arms. Not Louise.

First, I had to get her to the school. Transporting Louise there was an ordeal. The all but three minute car ride was traumatizing for her. She trembled and whimpered like the distress call of a fawn. She reluctantly passed through the heavy glass doors at the front of the building that bammed as they shut, smacking the metal latch. I either dragged Louise down the corridors to my classroom with her no-slip collar pulling tighter or carried her unbendable body.

Each evening Louise paced in circles and was stressed that she was forced to leave the safe haven of my home. I didn't like seeing her so uncomfortable in a new setting, but I knew it was for her own good. I was determined to figure out what made Louise tick.

Unraveling Louise's thinking, I instructed Barb not to pet her. Trouble was, reaching out and petting a dog was a person's first inclination. Louise perceived any extended arm as threatening. In her mind, that Boogeyman was reaching out to get her. Instead, as I requested of her, the janitor performed her cleaning duties and chatted with me while I prepared my lesson plans. The janitor basically stayed within earshot and made her presence known to desensitize Louise. Every now and then Louise was interested in who this alien was. Louise looked inquisitively at the custodian, but then her trust evaporated. Throughout the winter, more than three months, I took Louise back to school at least three nights per week. *Something's gotta click sooner or later*, I reckoned.

One evening in March, Louise reluctantly accompanied me to the school's office so I could make copies of worksheets for the next day's spelling lesson. Louise definitely wasn't singing "zippity doo dah" that we had left my classroom, which had become somewhat familiar to her by now. Nervous as usual, she occupied herself sniffing new scents in the work area. The copier machine hummed, spitting out papers.

Suddenly, the gymnasium doors slammed open with a thud. Whistles blew, balls bounced, and that ear-wrenching buzzer that signaled "game over" blasted the building. A crowd of spectators poured into the hallways as the school's after-hour intramural games ended. As if that wasn't bad enough, one of my third graders spotted Louise and shouted, "Look, Mrs. Cree has a dog with her!" The operative word was "dog." In seconds, a posse of children charged at us. Louise was in terror mode like I'd never seen before. She was unable to get away, nails slipping and sliding on the smooth, lucid floors. Louise's paws had no traction. Her appendages spread in every direction. Her belly dusted the mosaic tile. Her body flailed as she got on her feet and back-pedaled away from the crowd. "Please stop, kids," I beseeched. "Stay where you are. She's very scared. Try to remain quiet." Eager, youthful faces turned to frowning, disappointed grimaces. "I'm sorry. Don't come any closer. This one's a little different than most other dogs," I explained to the children.

I heard some of the parents mumble, "I've never seen a dog so scared as that one." Apologizing to the onlookers, I took the shaken Louise back to my classroom. She was paralyzed with fear. I felt like a fool. I should have known that basketball intramural games were scheduled. I hadn't spotted the cars in the parking lot since I pulled right up to the front doors, thinking it would be easier for Louise to enter the building. It was now my hope that we hadn't taken one step forward and three steps backward. With Louise, I figured it couldn't get much worse. Things could only improve.

Winter surrendered to spring. My scaredy-cat sidekick and I were nighttime regulars at the school. Parents, coming back to the school for PTA meetings or sports activities, noticed my vehicle in the parking lot, popped their heads in the classroom and asked, "What are you doing here so late, Mrs. Cree?"

Jokingly, I would respond to them, "I can't memorize my times tables, so I got detention." Louise quaked each time a new interloper poked a peek in my room. Barb continued to drop by my room on her breaks, sat on the carpet, and cajoled Louise with treats. Louise inched closer, gathering every ounce of courage in her flustered little body to advance toward the janitor. Many disappointing nights in those three and a half months followed where Louise would not take the treat from Barb, despite her gentle urging. Louise would get centimeters away, but didn't have the gumption to get close enough to accept the food. Louise's curiosity steadily piqued as she edged closer to her each night. Then, while I was busy making my morning chart for the kids, over my magic marker squeaking and the large, lined paper shuffling, I heard Barb cry out, "She took it!"

For what seemed like a month of Sundays, the bait finally worked! Louise gingerly approached Barb a few more times and gorged down the treats. I was so proud of my little girl's epic moment! Barb and I high-fived each other, danced with joy, and kicked up our heels. Our untiring efforts had paid off.

For the ordinary person, a dog taking a treat is no big deal. But for us, this was one small step for rehabilitation, one giant leap for Louise.

Beagle Bit

The top ten beagle names are Daisy, Buddy, Lucy, Cooper, Bailey, Snoopy, Max, Charlie, Molly, and Sadie.

Chapter Eight

Bringing Home the Bacon

Baby steps. That's how I looked at Louise's progress without going insane in the three and a half months since she arrived. Not only did Louise suffer from anthropophobia, fear of people, various other phobias from A to Z afflicted her. Webster's defines a phobia as, "an unreasonable, persistent fear of a particular thing." Louise owned a gamut of phobias. How about phonophobia? Take a guess – fear of noises. The world is full of sounds. And Louise jumped out of her skin at every little noise she heard.

One Sunday morning in April, I made Ray a good old-fashioned breakfast. What's this have to do with noise, you're thinking? Fluffy scrambled eggs, sausage, and bacon were the order for the day. Bacon was a rare treat in our home because of its fat content. Neither Ray nor I had high cholesterol, and I intended to keep it that way. Our menu also included cheese Danish, bagels, orange juice, and coffee. The works! The kitchen was a flurry of activity with the eggs cooking, coffee maker burping, sausage searing, and toaster oven ringing to indicate the bagels were a crisp, golden brown. The bacon sizzled and sputtered in the frying pan, spattering my stovetop with splotches of grease. Riley and BuddyLee, our canine garbage disposals, waited in the kitchen yearning for any morsel to drop as slobber hung from their jaws. They sat intently with their big, brown beagle eyes fixed on our platters. "This smells better than eating out," Ray remarked. Breakfast was his favorite meal.

Louise, drawn by the aroma, entered the kitchen but then surprisingly retreated. She dashed out of the doorway like a racecar driver taking off at the start line. Louise had always been food motivated. It was odd that she did not join the other dogs in soliciting the tasty spread.

"Where did Louise go?" I said to Ray. "Why did she run out like that?"

"Hard to imagine she's not here begging or expecting a tidbit to fall," he replied. "We'd better go check on her."

Ray found Louise stooped behind the corner of the couch, shaking uncontrollably. Mentally and physically, she was in a tailspin. Returning to check on the food, I struggled to carry her wavering body back into the kitchen. She leaped out of my arms, leaving scratches as her nails clawed my skin in her attempt to flee. I thought she almost broke her back when she fell and slammed to the floor. She ran from the scene as if the kitchen was a house of horrors. "Oh my gosh," I said to Ray. "It's the bacon. She's afraid of the noise!" We figured out the crackling and popping of the bacon sent her running like a frightened rabbit. We calmed her down by using deep massage to relax and soothe her. She slowly returned back to normal. Well, normal for Louise. We coaxed her with treats for almost an hour, stepping nearer to the kitchen and showing her it was safe to enter. She reluctantly joined us, after the bacon was done cooking, of course. Ray and I chuckled over Louise's peculiar antic with the bacon that day and finally sat down to eat our now cold, special breakfast.

Later that day Ray asked, "What's for supper?"

"Nothing," I replied. "I'm not cooking anything else today. After this morning, how about eating a bowl of cereal? Just make sure it isn't one of those crunchy, crispy ones!"

Ray deserved a nice breakfast. I owed the poor man a decent meal. I wasn't cooking suppers as much during the school week, with walking the dogs and correcting papers most evenings. The evenings I went back to school occupied my entire day. I wanted to cook for Ray and me, but I just didn't have the time.

"Don't go to all that trouble or dirty up dishes. I'll find something to eat," he'd say as I haphazardly threw a pre-packaged dinner into the microwave. Ray seldom objected, even when the fosters took precedence over other chores. He was a good man. I was lucky to have found such a supportive spouse.

Ray and I met briefly in October 1988, at a "Back to School Night" where I taught school. Then, that same year in November, at a Parent Teacher Conference, I said, "Come in and have a seat, Mr. Cree. You have a wonderful daughter. I enjoy having her in my class." We reviewed Alicia's report card, homework assignments, her classroom traits and her math skills. It was another busy year of teaching third grade for me.

One year prior to that, a high school friend of mine, whose son I had in class that year, said to me, "You ought to meet my brother." At the time, I was a single mother of Jessica. The following year, my friend's niece, Alicia, was in my class, and I did get to meet her brother, Ray. The rest is history. We dated and married in August of 1990, raising both of our daughters who were one grade apart in school. Ray later admitted that when he first met me at the "Back to School Night," it was love at first sight for him. We eventually moved to a home in the country. Twenty-four years later, we've raised our daughters together, have had a slew of foster beagles, and welcomed our first grandchild into the world. I am grateful to have an understanding husband who also believes in rescue work…that is a good thing with what he was putting up with having Louise in our home!

Ray took a backseat to the dogs lately. Louise was my life and my life became Louise. I neglected Ray as I showed the dogs more attention than him.

"You kiss those dogs more than you kiss me," he jested as I constantly smooched the pooches. But Ray was extremely understanding and encouraging with my rescue work. He joked that we needed to start a beagle farm and would have gladly adopted all the fosters. Despite the minor damage we've had – woodwork chewed, slippers eaten, couch corners peed on, lamp cords nibbled – Ray took it all in stride, made the necessary repairs, and never complained. He hardly griped about the dogs sleeping in bed with us, although our backs ached every morning. That's to be expected after sleeping with paws shoved along your spine. But that's not the half of it. We also tolerated fur up our nostrils and the inability to pull our covers over us because of beagle bodies weighing them down. What we'll do for puppy love! My poor husband tolerated so many inconveniences that he suggested we organize a support group for the husbands of Furry Friends Network volunteers. When he said that, I looked at him in a bantering way…and, he was not joking.

Down deep I knew that Ray felt he played second fiddle to Louise. I neglected his laundry, declined going out to eat, and didn't spend evenings watching television with him. I spent all my time obsessively researching dog behaviors to acquaint myself with Louise's challenges. I spent hours slumped over the computer as my tired eyes burned and stung, reading about canine phobias. Ray, my most wonderful husband whom I should have put first, was on a back burner. My main priority was Louise.

Louise became my little buddy. By now, three and a half months since she entered my life, I could approach her, pick her up, leash her, walk her, take her out to go potty, and cuddle with her. There were still times she kept Ray at bay. It took him twelve weeks of foster care to be able to get close enough to perform the simple task of feeding her. Many times she still did her 360s around the dining room table and he could not catch her.

One evening during that same month of April, Louise slept on the couch beside me in the family room. Her favorite spot was snuggling against the arm of the sofa. I tried to catch a glimpse of some television shows while I racked my brain formulating teaching plans for my third graders. My principal scheduled an observation of a lesson the following day. I concentrated on writing detailed instructions. Ray entered the family room. Louise popped one eye open, checking his every move. When Ray sat on the recliner, Louise went back to snoozing, assuming she was at a safe distance.

I was so involved in my schoolwork, I didn't notice that Ray brought down fingernail clippers and began to trim his nails. Suddenly, Louise jumped off the couch with a ghastly look on her face. She ran upstairs like someone probed her with a cattle prod. My papers, which I'd meticulously arranged in alphabetical order, went flying in disarray.

"What's wrong with Louise?" I asked Ray. "What upset her?"

Ray sat on the recliner dumbfounded as I headed for the stairs to check on Louise. Ray continued his manicure and "click, click, click" again was heard as he attended to his nails. Louise jerked and jolted.

"Don't tell me," I said in disbelief. "It's the fingernail clippers!"

"You mean those little silver snippers made her schizo?" Ray questioned.

"Do it again," I said.

Sure enough, Louise's wacky behavior was a direct result of the clicking. Ray got up and finished his manicure in the bathroom with the door closed. We just shook our heads at each other.

Any type of sudden, instant, or loud noise devastated Louise. The popping of a soda can tab, the clanging of a pot or pan, tearing aluminum foil, the whooshing of a trash bag, the whirring of the mixer, popcorn exploding in the microwave, a can opener buzzing, the computer printing, a door slamming, belching, you name it. Think about all the sounds you normally hear in your household every day. Really, think about it. Louise had a hypersensitivity to every one of them.

Most of our foster dogs, even if startled at first, became accustomed to daily noises and eventually disregarded them. At first, if the pup was originally kept as an outside dog, it was skittish and unsure of inside racket. My job as a foster mom was to desensitize the dog to everyday stimuli. Sometimes it was best to ignore the noise. I showed that I was not afraid of the sound. If I changed the trash bag, whooshing it to fit the trash can, I calmly walked away. Other times I allowed the dog to investigate the item. "See, this aluminum foil won't hurt you," I said, as a wary beagle smelled the silver cylinder. Then I'd gently tear off a piece. Counterconditioning followed with repeating the noise softly several times and providing reassurance until the dog did not react negatively. It worked with all of my former fosters…but not with Louise.

The main source of fear for several of our foster dogs was the many appliances in the house and their accompanying noise. It was amusing to see dogs view a television for the first time. They cocked their heads curiously at this machine with moving images on it. Hearing music, sound effects, human voices, and perhaps other animals was a novel experience for them. They barked as they wondered where the other person or animal came from. They could hear it, but they couldn't smell it. This baffled them.

They scooted away from the droning hair dryer or the humming and sloshing of the dishwasher. But they always came back to examine the foreign object with a quizzical look and that beagle nose sniffing. The toughest appliance the dogs had to conquer was the vacuum cleaner. I often waited a week or so after a new foster arrived to sweep my carpets. By then, my rugs had so much hair they looked like the floor of a barbershop. One foster beagle panicked and broke through my screen door when she was first introduced to the monstrosity. But usually within a few short days or several encounters, the majority of dogs adjusted to their new world of home sweet home. They became familiar with indoor auditory sensations. On the contrary, Louise's reactions were alarming.

Sounds were evidently magnified in Louise's head. One day when I crunched a Red Delicious apple, she flinched and bounded aback every time I took a bite. Each time I stirred my coffee too briskly and the spoon clinked the cup, she sprang out of the room like a kangaroo. Heaven forbid I drop a utensil on the floor. She couldn't get away fast enough. Her sense of hearing was on overdrive.

Anxious dogs like Louise are prone to phonophobia, also called acousticophobia, fear of loud sounds. Fears of unexpected or loud noises (loud noises referred to as ligyrophobia) are triggered by the orienting response, the brain's mechanism for awareness. When we hear certain sounds, the brain processes them to determine whether they might signal danger. Responding to sound is instinctive to all dogs, but Louise had her signals crossed. Processing sensory input keeps us alive and functional, but something was not wired correctly in Louise. She was in a perpetual state of high alert.

Since dogs hear better than humans, Louise heard thunder before I could. Her built-in radar system sensed an impending storm. She was attuned to changes in atmospheric pressure and static electricity. A cloudy, gray sky affrighted her. If we were outside, Louise couldn't get to the front door fast enough as thunderheads rumbled far away in the distance.

Hound dogs like Louise and herding dogs are more likely to develop brontophobia, fear of thunderstorms, and astraphobia, fear of lightning. Great. Louise had all these phobias. With these characteristics, the cards were stacked against me…and her. As soon as Louise saw a flash of lightning or heard a rumble of thunder, she shook like a leaf, whimpered like a lost lamb, and urinated. If the storm occurred at night, in a heartbeat she jumped off the bed and hid underneath it. Her tags rattled like a ring of skeleton keys. An offbeat chorus of jingle bells, coming from Louise's collar, interrupted my sleep. I could not coddle her, or else I'd feed into her fear. I distracted her with something positive, such as a toy, to redirect her and take her mind off the storm. *I don't feel like playing now*, Louise's panic-stricken expression told me. It never worked with her.

Up to 20% of dogs suffer from various phobias. Brontophobia, an abnormal and persistent fear of thunder that causes undue anxiety, is a common trait. It may be a throwback to when canines existed only outdoors. A thunderclap served as nature's warning to seek shelter. Louise gravitated to a corner or under a piece of furniture – her makeshift cave. She panted like she suffered asphyxiation. She dug at the rug, as if she had an imaginary bone, her nails polluted with carpet fibers. Some dogs become so destructive they would chew walls or jump through windows trying to escape. For the most part, we rode out the storm with Louise panting, shaking, and hiding until it was over.

Each time a storm concluded, I breathed a sigh of relief. *I'm glad that's over,* I thought, as Louise appeased herself. Often I took Louise on a long walk to diminish her anxiety level. It was the one thing she had grown to enjoy so much. Exercise releases endorphins in the brain and is a good stress reliever. Well, that is, until she heard the sound of a gunshot.

We live close to several hundred acres of state game lands set aside for hunting. It was not unusual to spot a flock of wild turkeys pecking the grass in my backyard, a red fox lurking in the bushes, and coyotes scrounging about in our hollow. A black bear once lumbered through our woods after he ripped down my neighbor's bird feeder with his massive claws, devouring tasty sunflower seeds. White-tailed deer, Pennsylvania's state animal, flourish in my neighborhood. Herds of them roam in nearby fields, grazing and glancing up as they keep a watchful eye for danger. When my beagles get on their scent trail, they bark and bay. The deer scamper away, white tails flagging up. Our area has a copious amount of rabbits hopping from under pine trees and squirrels scampering from telephone lines. Small game season invites an abundance of hunters to our surroundings.

One afternoon after a thunderstorm passed, I took the dogs on a walk. The bang, bang of a rifle sent Louise scrambling like she had been shot out of a cannon. She almost dislocated my shoulder as she pulled toward home, desperately trying to reach her safety net. My steps became three- foot strides as she thrust me forward. I struggled to keep control of the leashes as she dragged Riley and BuddyLee, our other beagles, like they were rag dolls. Her nails bled as they scraped the pavement, almost worn down to nubs. With each firing of the gun, fear swallowed her. Getting back home seemed like an eternity for the distraught Louise. The sole means by which I thought I could rehabilitate Louise - the walk – now had the potential to become another source of trepidation.

"Pop, pop" didn't always come from a gun. My neighbors held a birthday party outside for one of their young daughters. Parked cars filled their front yard while white tents and lawn chairs occupied their backyard. Kids ran about, the barbecue grill smoked, music blared, and streamers and colorfully-wrapped presents indicated a lively celebration. As the dogs and I walked by the residence, the timing could not have been worse. Louise ducked and cowered as she heard the sudden popping of balloons. It seems just as we went by, they held a water balloon contest. The children screamed when they got hit and became soaked. Pieces of red, blue, and yellow rubber hung to them as they shrieked with delight, wanting to gain retribution on the perpetrator. The balloons' explosions reeked havoc on Louise. This forced us to turn around, making the walk short-lived. We couldn't get home fast enough.

One time inside my home I made a terrible mistake, which only added to Louise's phonophobia, fear of loud sounds. This was entirely my fault. Louise fervently accompanied me out to the garage to unload groceries from my car, now dauntlessly passing that noisy screen door she earlier avoided…another small victory. Riley and BuddyLee eagerly jumped in the car like they were going bye-bye. The dogs loved snooping in the grocery bags, digging their noses in the hopes of snatching a pound of hamburger. I shooed the food mongrels from the rustling plastic bags as I put away the stash. They investigated the contents of the food cupboard in the garage, which is generally off limits to our dogs. They took advantage of its open doors, sniffing everything in sight, while I stocked it. When I was done putting groceries away, I misjudged the button on my car remote. Instead of pressing "lock," dummy me hit the "panic" button. *Oh, no, what did I do?* I thought. The blaring car horn echoed repeatedly in the closed garage as I fumbled to turn it off. My ears rang as the dogs howled and scurried to escape the shrill blasts of unbearable din. Louise skedaddled back into the kitchen with an abysmal fear even I hadn't witnessed previously. No wonder they call it the "panic" button!

Although the car remote incident was not an everyday occurrence, I felt helpless in conquering Louise's phonophobia. So what was I to do? Tippy-toe around my house, walking on eggshells? Was I to make it a sterile environment, afraid to cough, flush the toilet, operate a microwave, or slurp my coffee? My home was already low-key and quiet, compared to most. There were no babies crying their lungs out, no city life sounds such as horns blowing or traffic screeching, and no arguments or screaming matches ever erupted between Ray and me. How could Louise fit in the average household? Did she need a soundproof booth? Perhaps Louise had panophobia – fear of everything.

My grave concerns for managing Louise's phobias prompted me to request a meeting with Terri, the Furry Friends Network dog trainer, in person. We communicated through emails, but I preferred to have a heart to heart conversation to discuss the matters at hand. We met one Sunday in April at our local pet department store after one of our adoptathon events. This is where the Furry Friends Network volunteers showcase our available dogs and cats to the public. Of course, Louise did not attend. Terri focused on the zany stories I told about Louise's phobias. I took notes and listened attentively to her new suggestions to help Louise, writing my Louise List of Do's and Don'ts.

Terri determined at our meeting that Louise's issues should be addressed medically. It was time to consult one of our veterinarians who was specifically certified in behavioral problems. In spite of all my efforts, Louise needed to be on medication to calm her anxiety. Terri hoped this would give Louise that extra push to approach people, calm her reactions to noise, and probably decrease her frequent urination. I left our meeting having high hopes that with new strategies to implement, Louise may produce some positive changes. Maybe the medication was the answer we needed. I felt refreshed and rejuvenated. Just talking about Louise to someone who knew their stuff, getting sound advice, and going in the right direction for her treatment empowered me. Terri's opinion all along on Thelma and Louise was that their brains misfired too many stress hormones.

After our conversation, I went into the pet store and picked out a pretty, flowered, purple harness for Louise. I had read where perhaps the clenching and tightening around her neck with a no-slip collar just aggravated her stress when she was in terror mode. Made perfect sense. If I were scared and trying to get away, I wouldn't want something taut around *my* neck. At times, I thought Louise was going to strangle herself when she tried to pull away.

The next day I called Catherine Erickson, Thelma's foster mom, to share some behavior techniques that I learned from Terri. Catherine and I often emailed each other as well, comparing notes on "the girls" and celebrating the smallest bit of progress in their rehabilitation. We were in this together. We needed each other's moral support. Catherine was a veteran foster, like myself, but had never encountered a dog like Thelma…just like I had never encountered a dog like Louise. Catherine was equally frustrated with Thelma, who had not made even as much progress as Louise had.

"Why don't you bring Louise over for a visit?" invited Catherine. "Maybe it will do 'the girls' some good. They might remember each other. Perhaps Thelma will see how Louise lets you pet her. Maybe they'll even play together."

"It's worth a try," I replied. "We'll plan a date for the behavioral vet appointment, too."

A few days later, the visit with Thelma and Louise did not go as expected. It was pointless. Thelma paced in circles and showed no interest in Louise's presence. I was yet another stranger to Thelma. She ran like a feral cat. The only way Thelma could be caught or even approached was to throw a crate over her. Catherine was amazed that I could at least pick up Louise and pet her without a struggle. I could see she was disappointed she had not made the same amount of progress with Thelma. Terri told me that if both dogs had been fostered together, like originally planned with Catherine taking both dogs, Louise would have regressed and never made the "improvements" she had made with me. Fear begets fear. It was better the two were separated. Thelma's behavior was more than ten times worse than Louise's behavior. Louise was the more salvageable one. Thelma had more strikes against her. Thelma was heartworm positive and a fear-biter, not easy issues to overcome, even for an experienced dog handler. As scared as she was, Louise never tried to bite. I felt badly for Catherine, realizing the grim picture of Thelma's future. I counted my blessings that I picked Louise. I prayed for Catherine. I prayed for little Thelma. Rescuers, keep in mind we are volunteers, open up their heart and home to dogs in need thinking we are saving them and everything will go hunky-dory. Every foster will have a success story and a happy ending. Every foster will find its happy forever home. But that was not the case with Thelma and Louise. We had already experienced a rough road…and the rough road continued ahead of us. Sometimes rescue burns you out, but the good experiences far outweigh the bad.

Catherine and I made an appointment to take the dogs for an evaluation in mid-April. That was still almost two weeks away. A few days after we set the appointments, we both received a four- page survey to fill out concerning the dogs' phobias. We knew little about the dogs' backgrounds and upbringing, but we shared what we knew. I typed two pages of anecdotal records on Louise, mentioning her accomplishments on our walks, explaining her intense fear of people, her anxiety to noises, and her submissive urination.

And I was sure to include her unusual reaction to bacon cooking on the stove.

Beagle Bit

The main threat to beagle health is obesity. You should be able to feel your beagle's ribs, but not see them. Most beagles appear to always be hungry. Hence, people tend to overfeed and over treat their beagle. They are in denial when their beagle is overweight. Most beagles should weigh between 18 – 30 lbs., depending on body frame.

Chapter Nine

Louise on the Lam

The days leading up to April 13, 2006, could not come fast enough. It would be the start of school Easter vacation. I felt frazzled and worn out. There weren't enough hours in the day. Five days off from school was just the trick to catch up on housework, schoolwork, and have time to spend with Louise, not to mention taking care of my newest foster beagle, Droopy.

Yep, I did it again. I continued to scroll down those urgent messages on Petfinder™ for beagles whose time was up at shelters and needed out or they would be euthanized. I couldn't help myself. Fostering was in my blood, remember? With all the work of rehabilitating Louise, I knew she wasn't getting adopted for quite some time.

Call me crazy, but I picked another tri-color, handsome male beagle named Droopy who was around two years old. His picture screamed to me, *I promise I'll be good if you save me!* I showed Ray the picture of Droopy on the Internet. "Look at this one," I said to Ray. "He needs out. Can we get him?"

"Why do you always show me those poignant pictures?" he questioned. "Do you think I'd ever say no to a dog in need?" And so, Droopy arrived on a transport, stinky and playful, ready to be welcomed into the Cree household.

What's one more? I figured. The house was already a mess. The hamper overflowed with dirty laundry. The bathroom sink and tub had soap scum and water deposits that needed scrubbed with a steel wool pad. My car was a filthy mess with cinders stuck in the floor mats and dog hair trapped between the seats. The kitchen floor crunched as we walked on crumbs that needed swept. Normally, I was a tidy housekeeper. Actually, I considered myself somewhat of a neat freak. I hate clutter and some say I'm obsessed with cleaning. My house rarely looked or smelled like four dogs were in residence. But the duties of everyday life drowned me. My housework was ignored as I concentrated on working with Louise and keeping ahead of schoolwork.

Even my best efforts to keep up with schoolwork didn't prove enough. Any elementary teacher can tell you it is a constant battle to correct daily stacks of student worksheets. Uncorrected book reports piled up on my dining room table. Essay tests, which were time consuming to evaluate, sat in my briefcase. Fiction stories needed graded and journal entries required my response. Several hours of paperwork demanded my attention. Report cards were just around the corner. Who says teaching is a 9:00 a.m. to 3:00 p.m. job? It was all I could do to run a household, take care of the dogs, and fulfill my career obligations. I had big plans for this Easter vacation – to get my house in order, to make those piles of papers disappear, and to catch my breath!

April 13th was also an important date for another reason. Louise was to have her behavioral consultation at the vet. This vet had special certification and credentials in this area. Maybe Louise could really get the help she needed. Just like with people – a diabetic needs insulin, a depressed person needs antidepressants, an allergic person needs antihistamines. Maybe the medication would calm her nerves, ease her mind, boost her confidence, give her that edge she needed to meet humans, and lessen the incessant peeing. My first day of the spring break would start in a positive direction.

That first morning of spring break, I slept in until about 6:30 a.m., well, if you call that sleeping in. The extra half hour of sleep did me good. The dogs awoke hungry and ready to begin their day. They sensed our routine was a bit off the ordinary, as I did not rush to make coffee or run out the door to an early faculty meeting. Mommy got to stay home with them and they liked the attention. My new foster, Droopy, turned out to be an easygoing, laid back beagle. Things worked out well with him in the pack. Droopy and Louise entertained themselves playing with a huge, red and white braided rope toy. They yanked it back and forth, tearing fibers in pieces and dragging each other on the rebound. It was wonderful to see Louise amuse herself with the tugging of the toy, shaking her head like a shark with prey, pulling knotted threads in strands. She actually acted like a normal dog on occasion. This was the first time I could remember that she engaged in play with a doggy toy.

The remainder of the morning I spent multi-tasking. Organizing my chores to the fullest efficiency, I was very proud of myself. I threw in several loads of laundry, whipped up a batch of brownies, scrubbed the bathroom basins until they sparkled, and wiped that crusty kitchen floor. The dogs and I enjoyed a long walk because I didn't have to rush off to school. A stack of student papers got corrected and I had extra time to put fruit-scented stickers on them for the kids. Even though I missed my students, it was nice to have a morning of peace and quiet without the chatter of children - well, if you can call having four dogs at your house peaceful! After Louise's 2:00 p.m. vet appointment, I had plans to wash and vacuum my car.

To get there in plenty of time, I left home shortly before 1:30 p.m. For the first time, I decided to let Droopy loose in the house and not crate him. He seemed housetrained and did not bother or chew anything. He could use the pet door if he had to go out to potty. After their morning exercise, the dogs were sound asleep when I left. I assumed I'd be gone about two hours, three hours tops.

Louise shook in the car and moaned like she lost her best friend. Leaving the security of our house devastated her. I reside in a small town called Dauphin, which is located in a country setting fifteen minutes northwest of the capital city of Harrisburg, PA. I consoled Louise during the twenty-five minute drive to what locals call the "West Shore," which is across the Susquehanna River from Harrisburg. The office of Good

Hope Animal Hospital sits on the Carlisle Pike, in the suburb of Mechanicsburg, smack dab in the middle of the business district. The Carlisle Pike is a busy, five-lane highway. It is a highly congested area riddled with retail stores, strip malls, businesses, restaurants, fast food chains, car dealerships, and traffic lights.

Terri, the Furry Friends Network dog trainer, was gracious enough to take off work and meet me at the animal hospital. She was very interested in conferring with the vet and learning how to better treat Louise's intense fears. She stated that as a trainer, Thelma and Louise were the worst cases of dogs, shackled in fear, she had ever seen. She had never encountered dogs with such an extreme aversion to humans. Terri researched medications commonly used for canine phobia, and was leaning towards one in particular that studies showed produced good results. It sounds strange to give your dog "nerve pills" or "happy pills," as people call them, but when you own a neurotic dog, it may be the answer to your prayers. If something is wrong in the brain chemistry, as with Thelma and Louise, ordinary behavior modification is not enough. Thelma was unable to accompany us because Catherine, her foster mom, was unable to leave her job that day. Catherine took Thelma to the vet previously to treat her heartworm. But since Louise's behavior mirrored Thelma's, we could certainly provide valuable information on her to Catherine.

The vet intently read the questionnaire I brought with me, and the report I wrote about Louise. It didn't take her long to discover that Louise was an extremely fearful, unsocialized dog that exhibited mental abnormalities. Prior blood work done on Louise revealed no underlying physical problems. Her thyroid, kidneys, liver function, blood count, etc. all showed typical normal levels.

The vet watched Louise's behavior intently. We all sat on the floor to be less threatening to Louise. We did not make eye contact with her. We let her quivering little body approach us. Terri noticed that Louise was much more food motivated than Thelma. Louise peeked around the corner of the examining table. She got close enough to gobble a few treats from Terri. Terri saw that as a good sign. Maybe all the time I spent at school with Barb, the night janitor, paid off. We discussed Louise's phonophobia, fear of sound. I mentioned the example of Louise bolting from the kitchen when the bacon was frying. In all her years of vetting, the doctor remarked, "That's one for the books!" I joked that Louise suffers from phobophobia – fear of phobias! Louise had made some strides with me, I told her, but her success with the outside world was nowhere near as impressive. In fact, it was still troubling. The vet prescribed a generic form of an anti-anxiety drug. The next few weeks would tell us if the drug had benefits. Peeking inside the bottle at the little blue pills, I hoped that they would be Louise's salvation from her unhealthy mental state.

When our visit concluded, I needed eye drops for Droopy and waited several minutes until the receptionist could get them. Terri offered to take Louise out to go potty since she was so nervous and probably had to go pee. I really didn't think much of it. Louise wore her new harness and was in the competent hands of a dog trainer. After about five minutes, I went outside. Terri held the leash as Louise sniffed in the grassy area. To this day, I can't remember if it was I who yelled over to Terri or if it was Terri who yelled over to me, "Where are you parked?" It didn't matter. No one got to answer.

As this question bellowed out, Louise looked up and realized that I was not the one clutching her leash. She glanced up at Terri with that God-awful look on her face. All of a sudden she took a step back and panicked. In a split second, she completely slipped out of her harness like her body had been buttered. I couldn't believe what I saw! She ran as fast as lightning across the busy highway. I screamed in horror as she dodged in and out of five lanes of traffic, missing death's door by inches. Car horns blasted, brakes screeched, and rubber burned as the terror stricken Louise narrowly escaped tons of metal, which could have been her demise.

She wove in and out of commuters, some who were shouting, "Get off the road, you dumb dog!"

A motorcyclist suddenly changed lanes and almost caused a three-car collision to avoid hitting her.

A tractor-trailer blew its horn and swerved as Louise streaked across the freeway. I ran toward her in a crazed frame of mind, not thinking I could have met my own death.

"Don't chase her," Terri warned. "That'll make things worse. We've got to lure her to us."

Clamoring hysterically, I ran back into the vet's office, "Louise is loose!" Panic pierced me like an arrow. "Help me," I pleaded. "Louise got away!"

The startled vet workers jumped up from their duties and sprang to my aid. Surprised clients in the waiting room looked out the windows at the mass of vehicles roaring by. Pre-holiday Easter travel meant traffic was heavier than usual with cars lined bumper to bumper. One client felt my pain. "Oh, no, that lady's dog is loose on the Pike," he murmured to another patron.

Terri had already crossed the highway and was searching for Louise. "We've got to circle her back," Terri yelled to us. Terri knew what she was doing. As I crossed the road, a vet technician told me that Louise did return, again missing vehicles by centimeters. She scooted under a tractor-trailer and zigzagged her way back to the vet office. Some vet workers tried to corner her in a part of the property that was partially fenced, but Louise outsmarted them. She was as fast and slippery as a greased pig. And then a moment later, she vanished.

The posse spread out to look for her. Some of us had hopped in our cars, while others set out on foot.

We searched for hours. At every intersection, I had no idea which direction to turn. I combed parking lots of stores and restaurants, peering under parked cars thinking she may be hiding. I busted into fast food places along the Pike telling the customers that I had just lost my dog. Terri called the heads of the Furry Friends Network rescue, Robin and Shawna, to alert them to our situation. They promptly left work to help us. We walked to nearby residential areas, knocked on doors, and notified people of her description. Since it was the first day of Easter vacation, many children were off school enjoying the warm weather. Youngsters rode their bikes down the streets, squealing and popping wheelies, helmets and knee pads in place. Skateboarders jumped ramps, toddlers played on swing sets, and a lady walked, or rather was dragged, by her St. Bernard dog. *With all of this activity, Louise will be even more terrified*, I thought.

Spreading the word to anyone I saw, I informed them of Louise's fear issues. I talked over the buzzing of a lawnmower, waving my arms to get the person's attention, and informed the resident of Louise's disappearance. A group of kids, covered in soap suds, laughed and squirted each other with the hose. "No," they said, they had not seen her.

A guy worked on his car, leaning underneath the hood. "No," he said he hadn't seen her either. The only thing he saw was a dirty engine. I ran further to a construction site. A group of roofers, hammering away at shingles, might have a good vantage point, I thought.

"Did you happen to see a red and white beagle run by here?" I hollered up to them with my hands cupped to my mouth. They reported she whizzed by them a few moments earlier.

"She went thatta' way," they signaled, prompting me to run in the right direction, hoping I'd see a blur of cinnamon brown and white fur venture by. Huffing and puffing, my stomach panged and my legs could run no more. Feeling my age, my calves ached with weariness. I panted as I called her name, but Louise was nowhere to be seen. I couldn't believe how fast she traveled in so short of time. Those stubby little legs carried her at what seemed like the speed of sound, no doubt fueled by her fear.

Shawna eventually met up with me and got out of her car. Her face had that look that said, *Any luck?*

"I haven't seen her!" I yelled back.

Just then Shawna's cell phone rang. It was Robin with more bad news. Her car got rear-ended on her way over to help us. Months later I remembered this detail and felt like such a heel. I never asked Shawna if Robin was okay. You see, Robin had recently recovered from having disc surgery on her neck and had just returned to work. With my state of mind fully concentrated on Louise, I didn't think to ask if Robin got reinjured. Shawna, Robin's sister-in-law, jumped back in her jeep and took off in a flash. I honestly don't know if Shawna continued to look for Louise or rushed to aid Robin. I was too much in shock.

After that, I circled back to the vet's office to get my car. Perhaps there was a chance Louise returned there, looking for me. One of the secretaries told me she chased Louise down the highway with a net, but was unable to catch her. Drivers stared in awe as she hung out of her car window attempting to scoop the fugitive Louise. The little dickens was quick as a whip and evaded the swipes of the mesh. She catapulted away as this lady tried to nab her. Louise's escape had created commotion and mayhem during the vet's regular business hours. Workers dropped what they were doing to join the search. By now, the staff looked at me with dismay, knowing the high traffic volume of the area. With a dog like Louise on the lam, I had a slim chance of getting her back. Without it being said out loud, we all knew that.

By now dusk approached and the vet was preparing to close the office for the evening. Terri returned and reassured me that Louise would eventually tire out, hunker down, and find a place to hide for the night. "She can't keep running that fast, Sharon," Terri explained. "She has to be exhausted. Let's call it a day. We'll notify the proper channels tomorrow. I have to get home."

"You're right, Terri," I agreed sadly. Looking for Louise seemed futile. I didn't know which way to turn. Droopy was still loose in my house and all the dogs needed feeding. I decided to head home, make a quick supper, take care of the dogs, and come back to the area if it wasn't too dark.

Driving home in the car without Louise seemed surreal. When you go through a traumatic event, it's like your mind is playing tricks on you. It feels like it's not really happening, or it's happening to someone else as you look onward. I wanted it to be a bad dream and wake up. I envisioned Louise in the front car seat strapped in her doggy seat belt. I glanced down at her bottle of medicine. Never could I ever have imagined that this much-anticipated vet appointment would end in catastrophe. Repeatedly, I analyzed what happened and could only remember that horror look on Louise's face and that telltale, wrinkled brow. All she did was take one step back and *Poof!* She was out of that harness. Driving myself crazy over and over and over again, I still could not fathom how she maneuvered her way loose.

When I got home, I called Ray and told him the misfortune. Struggling to find the words, holding back tears, I felt responsible and guilty, humiliated that I let Louise down. Ray knew I was so upset and in shock that he didn't overreact or say anything to make me feel worse.

A man of few words, Ray simply stated, "We'll just have to find her. That's all. We'll get her back. She's out there."

Beagle Bit

Some beagles have ticking or freckles on their fur, especially on the legs, similar to a German Shorthair Pointer. This pattern is called mottled.

Chapter Ten

Louise is Lost

How could I have been so stupid? Louise was terrified of anyone other than me, I knew that. Why did I ever think she would be okay with Terri? Terri, even though she was a dog trainer, was a stranger to Louise. My carelessness had caused Louise's meltdown and escape. I replayed this incident a hundred times over and over again in my mind. Louise should have been transported in a crate. Her no-slip collar should have been put back on her, or I should have tightened her harness. I should have taken her outside myself to potty, or I should have waited until we got home, where she felt safe and was back to her normal routine, for her to go potty.

My last glimpse of Louise was that all too familiar terror in those penetrating amber eyes. I didn't have a clue how I'd retrieve her. Louise would never come to anyone else. It had to be me to find her. All the energy spent rehabilitating Louise seemed useless. I had cushioned her from the dangers of civilization. Now, she was out of her element. Louise had no mental armor to protect her from the world. Four months of helping Louise battle her fears were now lost. If I ever found her, I'd have to start from scratch. I failed her and myself as a foster. And, through it all, I just kept thinking, *poor Louise, out there all alone.*

Laden with guilt, I could hardly face Ray when he got home from work. We drove back to the vet's office to look for Louise that Thursday evening, hoping her trail was still hot. The car ride was silent except for my sniffling. Ray didn't say much but acted in a matter of fact manner and did what had to be done. We combed the construction site where the roofers were, meandered in and out of store parking lots, and pounded the sidewalks on foot. As of right now, it at least seemed that, luckily, she had not been hit by a vehicle on the Carlisle Pike and been injured, or worse, killed. We drove back and forth, performing the dreaded task of looking for her possible remains along the busy thoroughfare. When night settled in, I inspected underneath hedges and porches with a flashlight, hoping residents would not think I was a burglar. I prayed that Terri was right. Perhaps Louise found a place to lay low for the night, tuckered out. *Maybe she would be safe for tonight,* I thought. With glum, we headed home Louise-less.

On Friday, April 14, the very next day after Louise got loose, I reported her missing. I called everyone I could think of – The Humane Society, the local police department, the local township, the regular delivery people at the Post Office, all the veterinarians in the area – anyone who was out and about and may have spotted her or who might spot her in the future. Robin immediately had four hundred "Reward – Lost Dog" flyers printed with Louise's picture and description. She joined our efforts and took off work, handing them out to residents in strategic neighborhoods. The hunt for Louise was on in full force. The question remained, *would we ever find her?*

My long-awaited school Easter vacation went down the drain. The heck with the housework and schoolwork. They were of little importance now. Focusing on chores was vapid. So what if you could write your name in dust on my cherry tables in the living room? Who cared if the dust bunnies under the bed were the size of tumbleweeds? And we knew not to eat the food in the fridge that sprouted green mold. Besides, my concentration faltered as I corrected papers and couldn't figure percentages and average grades. My mind idled at ninety miles an hour with thoughts of Louise. My brain and body were in a state of high gear and confusion. Redundant actions were frequent occurrences. Absentmindedly, I put the cereal in the refrigerator and put the milk in the cupboard. Questioning why stains remained on my jeans, I washed a load of laundry… without adding the detergent. Then the mailman had to remind me to affix postage to the bills placed in my mailbox or they would come right back to me, unpaid. Thinking twice, I couldn't remember if I fed the dogs that morning. My mind was like a tangled ball of string and nothing could soothe my guilt or worry about Louise.

At 11:00 a.m. on the day after Louise went on the lam, I was supposed to be at a large local club membership store. I booked a table outside the store for raising awareness and much needed funds for our rescue group. This facility was always quite generous in letting non-profits sell food on the grill and our own pet-related merchandise at the entranceway. Organizations had to schedule this sale space months in advance. I was lucky to get us into this spot, especially on Good Friday, when I knew there would be plenty of shoppers. We anticipated the good crowds with people having off work and grocery shopping for their Easter dinner. I had assembled dog and cat Easter baskets, hoping sales would defray some of our costs for vet bills to run Furry Friends Network rescue.

Since I spent most of that morning on the phone, I arrived at this store late. Shawna, our cat lady and co-founder of Furry Friends Network, waited patiently for me. She had planned to meet me there that morning to assist with sales. Normally, I am a completely stable, responsible and grounded person. But I fell apart that day. In my forgetfulness, the tablecloths and power cord to run electric to the grill were left at home. The store, thankfully, let us borrow theirs, which got me off the hook. Our goods were not organized in my usual manner and the tables had a cluttered look. Furry Friends Network literature and brochures were scattered here and there. I slapped down hot dog condiments on the table haphazardly, making them spill. It wasn't that I didn't care, I did; I was just so pre-occupied with finding Louise and would have rather been doing that. Shawna commented on my disorganization.

"Sharon, get ahold of yourself," she said.

"I'm trying, Shawna. But I can't stop thinking about Louise," I blubbered.

At public events, I normally enjoyed conversing about the world of rescue. A positive interaction often resulted in acquiring more volunteers and foster parents to join our group and also more donations. But, I was so on edge that morning, I couldn't find the words. My faculties were in a fog. My muddled mind couldn't concentrate on matters at hand. I couldn't comprehend what patrons said, losing my train of thought. Bleary eyed, I made errors counting coins back to customers. I had to be careful not to shortchange them for their purchases. Although it still turned out to be a good selling day, I couldn't wait for it to be over so I could resume my search for Louise.

Ray and I spent the evening, as we would in the many days to come, looking high and low for Louise. By now the shock was over and reality had set in. Louise wasn't cuddled in bed with us at night, her feeding dish sat untouched, and I gazed in disbelief at her empty harness. Although Louise was micro-chipped, she had no identifying tags on her. They were still attached to the harness. The microchip was the only way someone could link Louise to us. But would Louise ever let someone get close enough to scan her? It was highly unlikely. Eight to ten million pets are lost or stolen each year in the United States. Fewer than 25% of them ever make it back home. With Louise, being found or returned to us was against all odds.

Later that evening, the odds seemed to turn in our favor. Robin called me around 9:30 p.m. to report that someone had spotted Louise. The woman got within three feet of her, but could not catch her. The lady said the dog she saw matched Louise's description, with the telltale splotch of white on her right ear. But as the would-be rescuer approached the frightened canine, Louise took off like a shot. The woman said she'd never seen a dog so scared. That is how I knew for sure that she had seen Louise. My poor baby must have traveled along a major highway to end up at the location where she was spotted.

When a few days passed without another Louise sighting, I grew desperate. Robin had an idea. She suggested we contact a pet communicator – someone with special powers who'd perceive Louise's whereabouts through spiritual means. At first, it sounded a bit ridiculous, but I figured I needed all the help I could get. Besides, what did I have to lose? I've always been a bit curious about the supernatural and intrigued by the paranormal. If anything might help us find Louise, I was up for the challenge.

The pet communicator was a compassionate and understanding woman. She gave me a shoulder to cry on and offered emotional support throughout our many conversations while Louise was lost. Offering her services for free, she did not charge fosters of rescues for her professional help. Our first phone call was one I'll never forget.

Skeptical at first, when I phoned her I half expected to speak to some mystical guru who sat crossed-legged and burned incense while clanging finger cymbals. Explaining my emergency, I did not give too much of an inkling of Louise. I asked if she needed me to mail her the harness so she'd have something tangible from Louise. She said she did not require it, that she relied on telepathy. After a few minutes on the phone, she told me she asked Louise what she missed about being away. Louise "communicated" to her that she missed her rope toy. Unbelievable! Remember that rope toy Louise and Droopy played with the morning she disappeared? That was the first time Louise ever played with a toy. Secondly, she asked Louise where she slept. Louise's response to her was, "My sage green pet bed." Chills shimmied up and down my spine. My toes tingled. My heart skipped a beat.

"What did you say?" I queried. When the pet communicator reiterated those words,

I thought I was in the twilight zone. Did she see Louise in her crystal ball? Louise slept in bed with us. Our entire bedroom – curtains, blanket, carpeting, and floral bedspread – is sage green. Not olive green, not lime green, not yellow green, not bright green, but sage green! How on earth did this woman know that? Of all the colors of the rainbow she could have guessed, how did she know sage green? She told me Louise was still alive and on the run, and that I would eventually get her back.

And so this began a series of phone calls to the pet communicator. She was a down to earth and honest person who I could easily talk to. I developed a rapport with her like she was my sister. It was one more avenue I used to locate Louise. This woman sensed my desperation and despair throughout the entire ordeal. She knew how much I loved Louise. Ray thought it was a bunch of mumbo jumbo and was a steadfast cynic, but this animal communicator made me a believer.

Ray stuck to the conventional methods of finding a lost dog. By Saturday, two days after Louise was lost, word was out to all the animal groups on the Internet about her disappearance. The S.O.S. call, "Missing Beagle, Please Help Us Find Her," was broadcast to sixty rescue organizations in our area. Zella Anderson, founder and head of the Central Pennsylvania Animal Alliance, was instrumental in coordinating communication in our rescue pact. Rescuers are a special breed of people. They are kind-hearted and forth-giving, and as with animals, never expect anything in return. Whereas most people were glad it wasn't *their* dog missing, rescuers acted like it *was* their dog that got loose. They quickly and graciously jumped at the chance to help. Advice from animal advocates flooded my inbox. Someone suggested using a dog whistle, but with Louise's phonophobia, fear of sound, I doubted if that would be successful. Another gentleman emailed me, telling me how he set up a barbecue grill where his beagle was lost. When the dog smelled the smoke's wafting aroma, he came running. *Not a bad idea*, I thought.

Ray and I spent the entire day Saturday, now two days after Louise's disappearance, scouring Mechanicsburg's suburban neighborhoods looking for Louise. We plastered telephone poles with big two by three foot, easy to read, foam board "missing dog" signs that could withstand the weather. We went in and out of stores, waiting in customer service lines for twenty minutes each to ask the manager for permission to distribute Louise's flyers. We posted placards on front doors and bulletin boards at vets' offices and the Humane Society. We revisited businesses along the Carlisle Pike and re-examined every nook and cranny along buildings Louise may have concealed herself in. It was a long, arduous day with negative results.

Sunday, April 16, was Easter Sunday. I traditionally entertained my relatives at my house since it was the roomiest. For most of the morning I prepared the holiday celebration, glazing the ham with brown sugar, hiding dyed eggs outside for my niece, and baking a coconut bunny cake. My actions that day were merely robotic, I just went through the motions. I was not my jovial self, but I didn't want to ruin everyone else's holiday. My mom and my sister Denise's family arrived. Dinner was at 1:00 p.m. Making the best of the meal, I put on a happy face and engaged in small talk at the dinner table. My appetite was suppressed because my stomach was in knots over Louise. Distracted and distressed, I picked and poked at my food. My fork scraped over the plate more than it shoveled food into my mouth. My mom noticed my lack of enthusiasm and my diminished appetite. Pulling me aside while we cleared off the table, she suggested, "Maybe you need to go on something for your nerves, Sharon. You can't afford to get skinnier. You're not yourself." I understood her concern, but I'm not one to reach for a pill. With a strong upper lip, I played a festive hostess and served dessert. With jubilance, I carried out the egg hunt for my niece, acting surprised at her momentous finds. By 3:30 p.m., I politely told everyone I needed to attend to schoolwork and not to worry about helping me wash the stack of fine china in the sink. Loading platters with leftover ham for my family to take home with them, I bid them a hasty farewell. By 3:35 p.m., I jumped in my car and sped over to Mechanicsburg, or should I say what we were now calling "Beagleville," with Louise flyers in hand.

By 4:00 p.m., I rang home doorbells hoping that I was not intruding or disturbing anyone's holiday meal. When I heard someone coming to the door, I hoped, every time, that this may be the one lead I need to finally find Louise. Adrenalin flowed as I pumped myself anticipating good news. Waving Louise's picture, I delivered a plea for my beloved pet. But within seconds, one by one, the heads of those who answered their doors shook with bad news, "No, I haven't seen her." My spirits withered.

"Sorry to hear about your dog," one person remarked as he glanced over at his own dog lying in the living room. What he really meant was, *I'm glad it is not my dog that is lost.*

Some people said, "I'll keep a watch for her," when they sensed my disappointment. Most people were kind and sympathetic to my plight. But after four hours, discouragement settled in. Saddled with sadness, I went home plagued by my thoughts of Louise's whereabouts and how she endured the last four days. *She didn't even get to eat any Easter ham*, I thought.

The next day, Monday, I gritted through my last day of Easter vacation. That day, April 17, I also completed a home visit with applicants interested in Droopy, my current foster dog. Some parts of life had to go on. Even though I loved all my fosters, I felt I shortchanged Droopy over the last few days because Louise was gone. Droopy was taken good care of, but I did not dote on him for those days with Louise missing like I did with my previous fosters. The time was not put into housetraining or exercising him on those days. My emotional connection with him was minimal during that time since I was so preoccupied with Louise's disappearance. Perhaps a part of me put up an emotional barrier so I would not get hurt again. Maybe I was afraid to love another foster dog while the hurt was so fresh with Louise getting loose…and the unpromising prospects of ever finding her. Driving to the potential adopters, I apologized to Droopy for my lack of attention. "I'm sorry if I neglected you over the past few days," I said to my beagle buddy sitting on the passenger side of my car with his doggie seatbelt securing him. That dear little creature looked at me as if to say, "That's okay. You've had a tough time of it lately." One thing went right that day. The home visit was a success. This family was later approved and would be adopting him. Droopy had found his forever home.

On the drive back, I couldn't let the day go by without looking for Louise. I memorized the streets of Mechanicsburg like reciting my phone number. Block after block, I drove for another three hours. My eyes darted in all directions scanning and panning yards, everywhere at once. I saw Louise's mug shot displayed everywhere. That poignant portrait pictured near and far. Poor Droopy sat in the car without making a peep. All of a sudden, he gagged and upchucked all over the front seat. All that driving made Droopy carsick. The smell of vomit penetrated my nostrils. "Yuck!" I shrieked as I combated to keep Droopy from eating his own regurgitation and watching the road at the same time. Needless to say, there was an abrupt end to the search for Louise and we headed home.

A fellow rescuer later phoned that evening to touch base with me. She was compassionate, but the bottom line was we did all we could possibly do at this point. Posters and signs were up, word was out in the rescue world, a "Lost Dog" ad ran in the newspaper, and all the authorities were contacted. Basically, she urged me to get back to my normal life. Half of me understood her opinion. In reality, Louise was missing five days now and I should accept the fact that she may never come back home. But the other half of me could not bear to give up. I could not sit back impotent at my house, resume my everyday existence, and wait for the phone to ring. Ray and I took a proactive stand from the start.

This was only the beginning of our crusade. We were determined to find Louise.

Beagle Bit

The Pocket Harrier was a close relation of the beagle, a toy version standing between 5 inches to 9 inches high. Fourteenth century hunters tucked them in their saddle bags or gauntlets. This Pocket Beagle became extinct in the 1920s.

Chapter Eleven

On the Lookout for Louise

It was now Tuesday morning, day six. I gave yet another idea a shot. With classes back in session, I phoned elementary schools in the areas where Louise was lost. I figured perhaps children may spot her as they walked to and from school. As a teacher, I begged the secretaries at other schools to make an announcement to the student body. "Please tell the students if they see a lost red and white beagle to phone me. She's a rescue dog and very scared of people. She needs her medicine," I pleaded. I thanked them, hoping I recruited more eyes on the lookout for Louise.

It was difficult, but I forced myself to return to school that Tuesday. I never played hooky in twenty-seven years of teaching, but that day I contemplated calling in sick. Usually a meticulous planner, I felt inadequate. That day I presented a lesson on the three branches of government in Social Studies, off-the-cuff, hoping my students couldn't tell I fudged it. My lesson plans for the week lingered on the table – unprepared. Materials and supplies I needed for class were not gathered. Using errors made from the children's worksheets, I wanted to reteach concepts that needed reviewing. But I had never settled down to grade the papers. Winging a lesson on geometry, I relied on my bag of tricks gathered from years of experience. The kids were excited to see each other after the holiday vacation. They showed off their new Easter outfits and were hyper from ingesting all that Easter candy. It was an unsettled, chaotic day. My nerves got the best of me. Teaching was my life, but right now my life seemed empty without Louise.

Every morning thereafter, I felt doom and gloom. The moment I'd open my eyes, I relived Louise's absence. It was hard to face each day without her. Ray did his best to pick me up from my doldrums. "Today's a new day," he'd say.

"So what's different about it?" I retorted. The realization hit me – this was not a nightmare, Louise might really be gone for good. I poured my heart and soul into this little beagle. In spite of all the aggravation and headaches Louise caused, I felt like part of me died. It was through the pain of this experience that I realized how much I loved that little girl.

For the next several days, the trail was cold. We heard nothing about Louise from anyone. It was like she vanished off the face of the earth. Each day I religiously checked the newspaper for a description of her in the "Found Dog" section. As soon as it arrived, I couldn't open the newspaper fast enough as my eyes searched for the words, "Found, red and white beagle." I realized I had created false hope. Who could even catch Louise if they found her? No wonder no one had answered the "Lost Dog" ad I ran in the newspaper.

Then there were two heartbreaking false alarms. Terri found an ad on a dog website about a stray beagle hanging around a garage. *No way*, I thought, *that was not Louise*. She'd never stick around people, no matter how hungry she was. The second was a message on my phone from the Humane Society of the Harrisburg Area. Someone found a beagle in the same vicinity as Louise. Fingers crossed, I was optimistic for a miracle. *Please be her and let her be okay*, I thought as I dialed the phone number with my trembling hand. My blood pressure skyrocketed as I counted the rings. *Answer the phone*, I ordered the unknown party on the other end. To my dismay, the lost beagle had already been claimed by its rightful owner. Hope had evaporated into continuing despair.

An emotional roller coaster continued for Ray and me. There were ups and downs throughout this entire time we were searching for Louise. We never gave up. We hung on for the ride of our lives. Many times I'd start my search psyched up, thinking this was going to be my lucky day. I visualized that precious picture moment where Louise appeared out of nowhere and ran into my outstretched arms with a field of daisies behind us. Instead, I would end the day so disgusted. There was also the reality that I had no idea whether Louise was still in Mechanicsburg where she originally got loose, or if she had roamed to another town. Beagles are known to follow a deer scent or a bunny trail and keep going. They are working dogs, scent hounds with stamina and endurance that can travel for miles. A statistic plagued me, 32% of lost dogs are found over ten miles from home. The hard facts were against my favor. Only about 16% of dogs and 2% of cats that enter shelters are ever reunited with their owners. Frustration ran high. At this point I did not even know in which surrounding suburb to look for Louise.

As if the emotional aspect weren't bad enough, my body suffered as well. I felt like a wringer washer smashed me. Every muscle ached. I dragged myself to school. The constant worry weathered me. All I wanted to do was sleep. Most people cannot sleep when they experience an emotionally stressful time. My body did the opposite. Even though I got plenty of shut-eye, I felt tired all the time. Fatigue could have ordered me to bed as early as 7:00 p.m. The mind and body work in mysterious ways. My mind couldn't handle the situation and tried to repress it through sleep. Maybe if I slept, I wouldn't think about Louise.

On the other hand, Ray was losing sleep. He ran our welding business working his usual twelve-hour day, then drove around for at least three hours every evening looking for Louise. He handled Louise's disappearance in his cool, calm, collected demeanor, but I knew he was hurting inside. We all know actions speak louder than words. Ray checked to be sure our "Louise Lost" signs were still up, stopped pedestrians to inquire about Louise, and visited the kennels at the Humane Society of the Harrisburg Area. Many nights he didn't get home until after 9:00 p.m.

One night, April 19 to be exact, now almost one week since Louise had been missing,

Ray came home with a worried look on his face. It was well past suppertime. I reheated his dinner so often that he needed a saw to cut the dry pork chops.

"Any sign of Louise tonight?" I questioned. "Dinner's cold."

"I saw something white lying on the highway," he replied quietly. "Roadkill. I turned around at the next exit but couldn't get a good look. It definitely had white fur."

"Do you think it's Louise?" I asked as my heart pounded.

"I couldn't tell. I need a flashlight," Ray answered. Ray grabbed a flashlight and made the twenty-five minute drive back to Mechanicsburg. It was an awful, rainy, miserable night. Lights from cars and surrounding businesses glared on the wet roads, it was hard to see. Visibility was poor. Ray told me later that he had to set the defroster on maximum to remove the condensation inside the windshield. The air had that rawness that chilled you to the bone. I waited an agonizing hour for Ray to return. *Please don't let it be her,* I prayed. Anxious for Ray's news, as the truck's headlights beamed through our living room bay window, I ran to the door. It turned out it was the fur of a white-tailed deer that didn't make it across the interstate. With a sigh of relief, we called it an early night and went to bed.

"I'm glad you went back to check," I told Ray. "I feel better."

"I could not have gone to sleep tonight not knowing if it was Louise," Ray said.

The not knowing was the part that drove us crazy. For six days now, we didn't know if she was alive, if she ran nonstop or hid, if she was sick, cold, or confused. We imagined her foraging through the meadows eating baby bunnies or field mice to survive. We had no closure. We always wondered about her. It ate away at us. Each time depression set in for me, Ray insisted, "As long as we do not receive word that she is dead, we will keep looking. There's always hope." That was his platform. That was my only salvation.

Ray's hopeful, upbeat attitude kept me going. In addition, many fellow rescuers, such as Gayle Kohr and Jan Zarick, joined our search. I made new friends and had a support group over the Internet. Months later, I met these kind people in person. They became my extended family. They knew the heartache of losing a dog. Many gave up their lunch hour and drove around looking for Louise as well. I warned them not to approach or chase her, making clear we were not dealing with your ordinary, typical dog. The goal was not to have them scare her farther away. If they saw Louise, I encouraged people to call me anytime, day or night. I needed to know she was still alive.

Catherine, Thelma's foster mom, offered to hunt for Louise. She knew all too well the minimal chances of getting Louise back. She stated her worst fear was that Thelma would jump her four-foot fence and she'd never be able to find her. A team of experts were deciding Thelma's fate. Thelma showed no progress towards humans. Catherine was unable to touch her in four months of foster care. Thelma paced in circles all day, devoid of human contact with Catherine. Thelma's quality of life was questioned. Was it fair to keep a dog of such severe maladjustments alive? Imagine what it is like to be in a constant state of terror. Compounding matters, Thelma had heartworm and was a biter. I typed to Catherine in an email, "It sounds harsh, but we got a raw deal. These dogs were social misfits, castaway critters, genetic inferiors, damaged goods. We attempted to alter behavioral defects in dogs that were biologically wired all wrong. And you can't change Mother Nature. We did the best we could for our 'two little beagles.'"

But, as I constantly reminded myself, I didn't do my best for Louise. I lost her. Even with Catherine and the others searching for Louise, we still had no new tips on her location. Four more anguishing days passed. I fretted over Louise day in and day out. Calling the pet communicator, I told her that we seemed to be at a dead end. She assured me that Louise followed a ten to twelve-year-old girl and was in the safety of her home. Perhaps this youngster resembled me since I am built small. Louise was very scared at that home and did not like the man of the household. But this family attributed her behavior to being a stray and being in a strange household. The pet communicator offered me a description of this house. This began another mission of knocking on doors that fit her account, rapping until my knuckles hurt. I explained my dire situation to the scores of owners of brick homes with a privacy fence that matched her portrayal. Perhaps I never saw Louise in my rounds because the six-foot fence blocked my view of the backyard. More disappointment ensued as I was unable to locate Louise at these residences. It didn't make sense; I couldn't imagine Louise following a human. This was the only exchange of ideas from the pet communicator that I doubted. It was funny though. This ten-day period with no word on Louise correlated with the time the pet communicator claimed this family had her. Maybe the family finally realized what a difficult and nutty dog Louise was. Maybe they decided not to keep her and let her go.

By now, ten days passed. We did everything within our power to find this lost dog, but our efforts proved fruitless. It was time to think outside the box. I remembered attending a Pet Expo to benefit service dogs at the Farm Show Complex in Harrisburg. Ray and I chatted with the Bloodhound rescue group and saw their demonstration. *That's it*, I thought, *if we could not find Louise, maybe Bloodhounds could!* This could be our answer. I spent most of that Sunday morning, April 23, on the computer and researched Bloodhound organizations. I would pay any fee, any price, to get Louise back. Money was no object. Charged up and eager to proceed with a new plan of action, I didn't care if I had to remortgage the house. It took several hours for the rescue group to respond to me. Another wall tumbled down. The local Bloodhounds were trained to rule out animal scents and only tracked humans. I supposed that made sense. The Bloodhounds would be going in every direction if they smelled every critter on the face of the earth. And so it was back to the drawing board.

How about contacting the local news station? We needed to get the word out to the general public, not just people in rescue. Somebody out there must have seen Louise by now. Radio stations would not announce her missing, no matter how much I begged. But I received an email from a fellow rescuer who was good friends with a local television news anchor. This anchorwoman was an animal lover and maybe had some pull at the station. I wrote a heart-wrenching, pitiful story to the news anchor about Louise and her escape. Explaining rescue work, I described how Louise could have died in a gas chamber, and also mentioned her medical needs. My story was so convincing that I thought any dog lover or human with half a heart would not refuse me. Another glimmer of hope soon diminished. Just when I thought the story would be considered to air, one of our adjoining neighborhoods suffered a terrible tragedy. Two junior high students were struck by a community service officer's vehicle as they crossed the street after attending a Friday night dance. One fourteen-year-old female student was killed, the other badly injured. The community was traumatized. The story was in the limelight for several days. A lost dog was the least of anyone's concern.

Finding Louise became an obsession with Ray and me. It permeated every thought, every waking moment of the day. Once while driving, I caught a glimpse of something white along the highway. Veering off the road, I almost hit the guardrail. It turned out to be a plastic trash bag tumbling in the wind. I was so preoccupied with finding Louise, I felt I was losing my mind. I wasn't walking my dogs as much, I wasn't returning to the classroom at night to do work, I wasn't cooking. Ray and I worked our full-time jobs and dedicated the remainder of each evening searching for Louise. We collaborated on our daily plan of attack, dividing our individual stomping grounds. We combined forces and assigned tactics in the quest for Louise. One day after our jobs, we both drove a total of nine hours exploring regions she may have traveled. Mission Impossible turned Pet Detective at Large.

As if things weren't bad enough, in the midst of Louise missing, I received a disheartening email. As soon as I saw an email from Ranger's owner, I figured it was trouble. About a year earlier, I rescued a beagle named Ranger. He spent five months in a shelter and was scheduled to be euthanized. After I fostered Ranger, a male schoolteacher and his son adopted him, but Ranger had a hard transition in his new home. At first, I received several complaints about his destructive habits, potty accidents, and aggression towards other dogs. None of these characteristics surfaced while in foster care at my house. Ranger had a rough start, but we ironed things out. Now the man wrote to tell me he started a part-time business that kept him away from home long hours. The son evidently lost interest and did not keep up with his part of the bargain in caring for Ranger. The novelty of owning a dog wore off. He wanted to return Ranger to Furry Friends Network. As per our adoption contract, the dog comes back to the rescue. I made arrangements to pick up Ranger later in the week. Even after carefully scrutinizing applicants, you never know what the future holds. Of all times for this to happen. My world came crashing down.

Maybe the Man Upstairs knew I was at my breaking point. On Monday, April 24th, now eleven days after Louise went missing, we received encouraging news. Each day after school I rushed home to check the answering machine. Flying in the door, I did not acknowledge the dogs by giving them their pats on the heads and hugs and kisses. I ran straight to see if the light was blinking. The red light winked. It was the message I had been waiting for! Lo and behold someone spotted Louise! A bartender drove home from his shift at 3:00 a.m. He saw a little dog with no collar who looked very scared. He got the impression it had been dumped along the road. The dog hovered in the bushes along Lamb's Gap Road, a wooded, winding, narrow, two-lane street in Mechanicsburg. The man did not stop to get the dog. But after seeing my "Lost Dog" ad in the newspaper, the bartender concluded it had to be Louise. When I spoke to him, I could not thank him enough for phoning me. Despair turned to relief as I restored my vigor. Louise was alive and still out there.

Plan B was quickly put into action. Now that we had a recent sighting, we needed to establish a reliable food source to keep Louise contained in that area. A mass email followed to fellow rescuers in that vicinity to put food out for her. Even though a raccoon or opossum could snatch it, Louise had to be starved by now and the food would lure her. I didn't want her traveling farther in search of food. She had already traveled a few miles from the vet's office and crossed Interstate 81, a high-traffic six-lane highway, to get to this new destination. My worst nightmare of this whole situation, if I could even pick one, was Louise spending the last moment of her life in horror, staring at the oncoming headlights of an eighteen-wheeler, speeding towards her. All she ever knew in her life was fear. It tore at my soul to imagine her last seconds on earth with this sensation.

Since I knew Louise was still alive, I could hardly concentrate at school the next day. My lessons felt monotonous and lacked rhetoric. Watching the clock continuously, I counted the minutes until dismissal at 4:05 p.m. After school, we teachers tidy our rooms, use the copier in the office for the next day's worksheets, and discuss our day with the kids. My mind wasn't on school that day. I jabbered about Louise in my overwrought manner. Sensing my despondency, a co-worker suggested I take off the next day.

"You have the sick days. Use them," the other third grade teacher suggested.

"If it was my dog, I'd do it," interjected the second grade teacher as she put up her class's artwork in the hall. "The kids will survive a day without you."

Then the Learning Support teacher remarked, "If anyone can find that dog, you can, Sharon." I was a bit surprised by this comment. I really never considered myself any type of dog expert. I realize I am an animal aficionado, but my own dogs don't even know many tricks. Maybe this teacher knew the dedication and commitment I had to teaching. I loved my foster dogs with that same passion.

So I took their advice and played hooky for the first time in my lengthy teaching career. I called in sick (well, *sick with worry* was true) on Wednesday, April 26, now thirteen days that Louise had been on the loose. I felt a little guilty fibbing to my principal, but it was only partly a fib, I was not feeling very well. I also thought it was best for the students since I was there in body, but not spirit lately. It would all be worth it if this were the day I would finally find Louise.

Once again, I started out on my search excited and optimistic. But it was late April. Many of the back roads were filled with thorns and heavy brush. Spring rains in central Pennsylvania sparked thick foliage. It was often damp and cold. There was nowhere to park the car on the tight, two-lane shoulderless roads. Dense vegetation prohibited me from seeing a few feet past the guardrails. Packed undergrowth obstructed my view. Briars hanging every which way hampered my observations. Returning home hours later, I had an empty hand, an empty heart, and an empty tank of gas - another excursion devoid of Louise. She could have been hiding anywhere.

That's it! My revelation occurred when I finally realized that little stinker must have been hiding during the day. No wonder we never saw her. The two reported sightings we had of Louise occurred at night. All those people searching over their lunch hour never saw her either. Louise was too scared of people and noises to be out and about during the day. She became nocturnal. She moved at night when it was safer to search for food.

This is how she was surviving, I was sure. Robin, our Furry Friends Network president, told me from the start that Louise was street smart. That warped little mind of hers wasn't so twisted after all! Louise was a survivor. Robin knew that. Robin had an uncanny ability to perceive and gain understanding of all the dogs in our rescue. Even though she was not the actual foster mom, she had insightfulness about each dog. Robin, who had limited or no contact with a dog, had powerful gut feelings about it. She was quite dog savvy. Her intuition amazed me. She was sure we'd get Louise back. It would just take time.

It was time for me to think like Louise. I knew her habits and her fears. Of course she shied away from the hub-bub of activities during the daylight hours. I approached this search all wrong. Louise retired during the day and lurked at night.

By golly, I was going to find that little escape artist if it killed me.

Beagle Bit

The tip of a beagle's tail must be white or he is not considered a beagle. The white tip or flag has been selectively bred into the dog to make him visible when his nose is to the ground.

Chapter Twelve

Operation Louise

Now that I started thinking like Louise, how was I ever supposed to hunt for her at night? Dress like a Ninja, sneak through backyards and prowl through parking lots? If I had to stay up all hours of the night, teaching third graders all day would be impossible.

My languid body couldn't sustain it. Sitting at my computer, I started to contemplate how I could outsmart Louise. If I couldn't get to her, maybe she would come to me. I reviewed the list of hints and suggestions sent to me online by my concerned co-rescuers. "Set up a dog trap," one pet sleuth advised.

A dog trap. Somewhat dubious, but I was game, although I had no experience using a trap. My mom once hired a pest control company to set live traps in her yard to catch nuisance groundhogs. The traps were successful with little interference from humans other than supplying bait. The groundhogs remained unharmed and were transferred to a more suitable habitat.

Louise was now on the lam for two weeks. Excited with this new solution, I called Robin. "It's a great idea," Robin admitted, "but Furry Friends Network doesn't own a trap." Robin wasted no time sending out a mass email to fellow rescue organizations explaining our dire situation. We needed to borrow a trap and get it in place as soon as possible, as we had a recent sighting of Louise. My extended family of rescuers pulled through again. That same evening, I received a gracious offer to lend us a trap. But it would not be available until Saturday. It was Wednesday, that meant three more days to wait. And three more nights before the trap could be set. A restless night followed as I tossed and turned in my sleep, envisaging Louise in the mechanical device. *Would she ever take the bait?* I wondered.

Before 6:00 a.m. on Thursday, April 27, I was awake, still worried about Louise, but anxious for the days to quickly move to Saturday when we would be able to set the trap. I arrived at school earlier than usual to review what my substitute accomplished the day before when I was not at school. Concerned about my well-being, the kids asked, "Where were you yesterday, Mrs. Cree? Were you sick?"

"I had a terrible case of laryngitis," I told them, putting on a hoarse, raspy voice. (It was only a teeny, tiny white lie.)

On my desk, a hand-made "Get Well, Mrs. Cree" card greeted me. There it was, the first thing I noticed, lying on top of all the day's papers. Inside was written, "To our favrit teacher. We misset you. Hope your felling better," by one of my mediocre spelling students. A female stick figure that resembled me was lying in a pencil-lined shape of a bed. A stick thermometer protruded from my stick figure mouth. "Help me, I'm sick," moaned the patient as these words appeared inside the picture's speech bubble. Beads of sweat were drawn rolling down my face. Shame on me for being dishonest, my conscience told me. God will get me for this. Watch me really get an awful bout of strep throat. What I really wanted desperately was for God to bless Louise and return her to me, safe and alive, even if she would still be scared. How I prayed for that to happen, the sooner the better.

Although my class loved good ol' Mrs. Cree, another typical day of instructing third graders followed. One boy had a nosebleed all over his science quiz. "Pinch, pinch," I shrieked in my forced "I have a frog in my throat" voice as droplets of blood spattered on his test paper. After I sent him to the school nurse, another little girl tattled that a classmate was being mean and would not be her friend, so the bully had to write an apology. At lunchtime, a girl spilled chocolate milk all over her new dress. She expected me to say "abracadabra" and put it in an imaginary washing machine. While chewing on his sandwich, another child lost his tooth and probably swallowed it. He cried because he did not have it to put under his pillow for the Tooth Fairy. It took all my patience to deal with the tribulations of that day. After counting the hours for the workday to end, when it finally did end, I jetted home to check the messages on the answering machine. No flashing light. No Louise. Once again, that melancholy mood cast over me.

School exhausted me so much that day, I didn't feel like driving over to Mechanicsburg to search for Louise. This was starting, even to me, to feel like a wild goose chase and I would have to drive all evening resuming the search. Tonight, I just didn't have it in me. My strength was sapped. Besides, I spent the previous day and evening looking for her. There were no more stones to turn over to find her until I could get the trap.

Deciding to stay home, I cooked a nice supper for Ray, spent time with my own dogs, Riley and BuddyLee, and foster beagle, Droopy, and worked on lesson plans. Maybe one night, at least, should be normal. What a pleasure it would be to actually watch television, read the newspaper, or do some gardening. Yes, I said to myself without needing too much convincing, I needed an evening just for me. Restoring my regular routine, for one night, would be a welcome change.

At 6:30 p.m. Ray phoned before he left his welding shop for the day. He customarily called to ask if we needed anything, such as bread or milk, from the store.

"How was your day?" he asked.

"I don't want to go there," I said. I also felt like adding, "Why did I ever become a teacher?" But instead I said, "Let's skip looking for Louise just one night. I'm beat. Since I made a decent meal, let's eat supper together."

Ray agreed, admitting he had a hard day as well and looked forward to relaxing and unwinding in his recliner.

As we discussed our plans for an evening at home, the call-waiting signal beeped. Not wanting to be bothered by anyone, I hesitated switching over. "Hold on a second, it's the other line," I said.

"They'll leave a message," Ray said.

"Maybe I'd better get it," I answered as I remembered Louise's Lost Dog ad was still in the newspaper. Ray and I said good-bye. He'd be home soon. I clicked over to the other line.

"Are you tha' lady with tha' missin' beagle on tha' big posters?" a strange voice inquired.

"Yes, that's me," I replied, still confused as to who the other party was with this southern drawl. My heart quickened.

"Well, I seen her last night. She was behin' the dirt piles in the cemetery off Wertzville Road at one thirty in the mornin'. She's sure a scared littl' thin'," the man remarked.

"A cemetery? Wertzville Road?" I exclaimed. "I'm on my way! Thank you!"

That phone call from the caretaker triggered the plan I deemed Operation Louise. Almost forgetting to turn the stove off, I dashed out the door. In a split second, I loaded up the car with the beagles Riley, BuddyLee, and Droopy. Maybe Louise would hear them bark or smell their scents. Maybe their hound dog noses would track her to me. Now we had the proper location in which to set the trap. The newly designated "Beaglemobile" screeched out of the driveway. Neighbors doing yard work glanced up with that *Where's the fire?* look on their faces. When we rounded the corner of my street, beagle bodies slammed against the car's vinyl interior thanks to the physics of centrifugal force. Twelve paws regained their footage as my car careened the curve. Six beagle ears flapped in the wind as I accelerated the gas pedal speeding towards Mechanicsburg.

Wertzville Road was another hilly, winding, two-lane highway, if you could call it that. It was a main road that linked Mechanicsburg with the small city of Carlisle. On the other side of the road sat a mountain. It was easy to gain speed on the steep road mounds as the curves approached without much warning. Passing the cemetery, I squealed my brakes to slow down and then turn around to go back to the entrance. Adjacent to the cemetery was a small, mountain stone church. Its beautiful white steeple towered the grounds. I circled the property three times. Granite tombstones and bouquets of flowers dotted the level land. A cast iron liberty bell was mounted on the front lawn. What an ironic symbol considering Louise's unwanted liberty. Two large piles of dirt stood in the rear.

Heaps of earth overshadowed me as I parked my car. The dogs were on their leashes and bolted out of the car barely before I had my door open, pulling me along with them.

They had a field day exploring and sniffing new territory. *Arrrrr, arrrrr,* baying exploded from these three beagles as we probed nearby woods, chasing out a bunny from under the brush. Noses to the ground, they pulled me like a tugboat. BuddyLee, typical male dog, lifted his leg at least ten times on the headstones, tinkling two drops here and there to mark his territory. Riley ate a vole in one gulp. And Droopy devoured rabbit turds like they were caviar. Tracking hounds they weren't. Too many interesting distractions. *At least we put our scents down for Louise,* I thought. The dogs roved through the surrounding bushes as three white-tipped tails surfaced above their deep, throaty bays. We unknowingly ended up in someone's backyard that bordered the cemetery. By now it was 7:30 p.m. and starting to get dark. A porch door slammed. A woman in her thirties came out to investigate why I was trespassing in her yard with my slew of scent hounds. *She's going to give me heck,* I thought

"Excuse me, ma'am. I apologize for being on your property, but did you happen to see a little lost beagle around here?" I asked in my most polite voice.

What a relief when she answered, "My husband saw a little dog hiding in the pine trees last night. The dog wouldn't come to him."

"Did she have red fur?" I asked hopefully.

"He didn't really say, but I'm not sure he could see its color, it was dark," she replied.

My new acquaintance listened in awe as I pattered the whole saga with Louise to her. Her eyes widened, mouth dropped, and she shook her head slowly side to side as I explained Louise's adventure. "I think this just may be your dog," she said.

"Can I come back to your home another night?" I asked. The lady told me that her family had a vacation planned for the upcoming weekend. They were packing up the camper and leaving tomorrow. An RV parked in the driveway had its windows opened for fresh air, scrubbed awnings rolled down to dry, and kids' bikes fastened to the rear. She invited me to hang around and stay there as much as I needed while they were away. She permitted me to use her deck and set up my lookout in her yard. We then walked over to the area under the evergreens where Louise sheltered herself. A few feet from the trees sat a blue ceramic dish with a mushy light tan substance.

"What's that?" I asked.

"There's been a stray cat hanging around here for the past three weeks. He's even declawed. He has to be someone's cat, but I've had no luck finding the owner," she replied. Feeling sorry for it, she provided its daily meal. Perhaps this reliable food source kept Louise lingering here.

My streak of luck flourished. She introduced me to her neighbor who lived across the street. This woman was also in rescue and offered assistance. Ginger Poffenberger volunteered with the Susquehanna Valley Collie & Sheltie Rescue. I informed her all about Louise's stunt and what kind of dog we were dealing with.

"I have a sheltie that's really scared, too," she told me. "I couldn't imagine what would happen if he got away."

"You have no idea what my husband and I are going through. Thanks so much for your help," I told her genuinely. It was encouraging to have another comrade in my task force, especially since I was naïve with setting a trap. I told her I'd be returning with one on Saturday.

My three beagles and I left my newly found friends' backyards and headed through the cemetery to the car. It was now dusk. I piled the dogs into my car as I stood by the driver's door, sighed, and studied the mountains of dirt in the cemetery one last time. Then, a prodigy befell me. Louise appeared from the brambles. *No, that can't be her. This must be a hallucination!* I thought. Being so tired from my rotten day at school, perhaps my mind played tricks on me. I shook my head to make sure I wasn't dreaming. It *was* her! She emerged for a moment, but upon seeing a human, she hightailed back into the bushes. She didn't know it was me. I recognized her caramel brown fur, that crouched posture, and that tail curled under her behind. This was real. *This was Louise!*

Hurriedly, I dragged the dogs out of the car and ran over to the area. We tried to walk quickly on a dirt trail that led to a ravine by the road. The vegetation and steep incline made it almost impassable. "Mum, mum," I coached in a soft voice hoping she'd recognize our signal. I didn't want to scare her away. The mountain looked down at me as if it could swallow Louise. *If she crosses Wertzville Road, I'll never find her,* I thought. "Louise, it's me," I pleaded. Then I tried, "Go for a walk," in my inflected tone thinking she'd respond to her favorite activity. Hearing those words, the beagle brigade charged onward. We soldiered through poison and hawthorns. Burrs invaded my clothing. Suddenly Riley's barks turned to yelps. As Riley looked up, barbs were stuck all over his face. I lost precious time as I stopped to pick them off. They clung to him like Velcro®. We surveyed the area until dark, but Louise never reappeared. We boomeranged our way back to the car. Deserting Louise, I had no choice but to go home without her.

When I got home, Ray couldn't believe I spotted her. "How in the heck did she get that far without being hit?" he wondered. Louise was now almost five miles from where she first got loose at the vet's office on the Carlisle Pike. That she survived was amazing in itself.

"She must have crossed the interstate to get there," I confirmed.

"It's short of a miracle," he said and shook his head in disbelief.

With confirmation she was still alive, we had renewed hope. Over two weeks had passed since her escape. Robin was right. She was my little survivor. She was my Louise.

"I saw Louise last night," I smiled as I told my principal when entering school that next morning. We hugged each other and rejoiced. Dancing like the scarecrow in *The Wizard of Oz*, I jumped and clicked my heels down the hallway. I hollered, "I saw Louise!" into every classroom as I flitted down the yellow brick corridor making my way to Room 109.

"That's great," the first grade teacher said as I startled her. She dropped her pencils, causing them to scatter like a box of toothpicks.

"You'll get her back," replied the second grade teacher as she turned on her laptop.

"I'm so glad she's alive!" exclaimed my teaching partner as she hung the date on her calendar. "We're pulling for you, Sharon!"

A great day of learning ensued. I was high on life! Much better than the day before, exhilaration bubbled out of me as I delivered my lessons with gusto. We learned fractions, our bean plants sprouted, and everyone passed the quiz in Social Studies. It was a productive day, the kind of day that made me glad I was a teacher. And when I left school, I felt one hopeful step closer to finally bringing Louise home.

But first, my foster dog, Droopy, was getting adopted. The approved applicants and I met after school that Friday, April 28. I said good-bye to my four-legged friend. This family was a good match for him. He'd have fun playing with his new canine sister. Another beagle saved, another beagle went to his *fur-ever* home. Mission accomplished. Now, back to Operation Louise. Without stopping to eat supper, and with renewed hope, I scudded over to the cemetery to once again look for Louise.

For two hours, I sat in my car until dusk, parked in the family's backyard, facing the cemetery. Waiting and watching, my eyes zeroed in on the outline of the pine trees and the piles of dead needles that lay underneath. With intensity, I listened for any footsteps detecting movement or Louise's unmistakable bark. Darkness settled. Silence screamed as I gazed out into the blackness. All I could see now were the silhouettes of nature. The quiescence sedated me. My head bobbed as I dozed in the driver's seat, sleepy from an emotional week. All of a sudden, I awoke with a jerk. *What was that*, I thought. A shadowy figure pounced on my car hood and inched up the windshield. My neck snapped with whiplash as I jolted up from my slumped position. My heart's arrhythmia vibrated my entire body so strongly that I was sure it was heard for a mile. A furry paw batted my hair through my open driver's window. A screeching meow pierced my ear.

Oh, it's only you, I thought. Once I realized it was the stray calico cat that I heard about the night before, I got out of my car and greeted the furry feline.

This affectionate stray cat wove in and out of my ankles as I stumbled around the yard. Walking around the perimeter, I called for Louise. With each step, the cat hindered my movement. He wouldn't leave me alone. He slithered in and out of my legs, causing me to tumble, landing palms first, in the grass. "Friendly little thing, aren't you?" I said to the calico creature. "But you're impeding my efforts." His relentless rubbing became a hazard. "Shoo," I chided as I swatted him away with gentle strokes. It was no use. He was sure he'd made a new best friend.

Since my serpentine sidekick hampered me, I remained stationary. Fearing I'd trample the poor thing, I found a spot in the family's backyard, which bordered the cemetery and planted myself there. Armed with my blankie and flashlight, I set up a lawn chair at my lookout post. Still as a sentry, I tarried until after 11:00 p.m., scanning the hemlocks with my mini searchlight. The kitty snoozed on my belly, which growled from hunger. I shouldn't have skipped supper. Above the sound of gastric juices gurgling, I heard a rustle in the woods. *Could it be Louise?* Two red, slanted eyes glistened as my flashlight beamed them. An opossum sported its jagged teeth, snarly snout, and clenched claws at me. It crept closer and then slinked away into the night. Owls hooted and raccoons roamed as nocturnal life emerged. Around midnight the heebie-jeebies got the best of me as my mind envisioned *Dawn of the Dead* corpses rising from their graves. Protecting my jugular from a zombie attack, I pulled my blankie higher, clutching it around my throat. Bats squeaked and swarmed above my head. *What if they're rabid*, I worried. By then, my empty stomach nauseated me. I couldn't last through the night.

Enough of this, I thought. So much for Survivor 101.

Sadly, there was no sign of Louise that night. I would have to come back tomorrow.

Beagle Bit

A group of beagles is called a bugle.

Chapter Thirteen

The Stage is Set

Operation Louise was in full swing on Saturday, April 29, now sixteen long and worrisome days since Louise was on the loose. First thing in the morning, I picked up the trap from another rescuer. "Good luck with this. I hope it works," said Linda Corson of *AngelPets.org*.

"This is our last resort," I told her. "Maybe with divine intervention, we'll get Louise back." Having my doubts, I studied the steel cage. Louise disliked being crated. *Louise would probably have a better chance getting struck by lightning than entering this trap,* I thought with pessimism. *But maybe if she's famished enough, she'll go in it.* I forced myself to think positively.

Arriving back in Mechanicsburg at my observation post, Ginger, from the sheltie rescue group, helped me set the trap. I printed the words "Property of Furry Friends Network, Do Not Disturb" with my name and phone number on the large identification tag enclosed in plastic and secured it to the trap. Since Louise may not like walking on the wire, I placed a blanket on the cage's floor. We tested the spring-loaded pedal. The trap shut with a vengeance.

"Should we leave it out at night?" I asked Ginger.

"If she's moving at night, you'd have to," replied Ginger.

"But what if I catch a skunk or some other varmint?" I questioned.

"That's your problem. See that back door?" Ginger said with a glint of humor in her eyes. "Open it and run!"

With those words of comfort, I feared the outcome. What critter would I catch? With all of the possibilities out there in the open country, only one of them being Louise, this was a long shot.

However, I employed several other tactics to especially lure Louise to the trap. Fellow rescuers advised me to place any articles familiar to Louise near the site. Drawn by scents she'd recognize, I positioned her pet bed by the trap. Plush dog toys and bone-shaped rawhides were scattered under the pine trees. The scene looked like a doggy daycare. I had dug through my hamper and chose pieces of my stinkiest, dirtiest clothing to set around the area. Dingy socks, a Penn State sweatshirt with coffee spilled on it, and my jeans with mud on the knees were strategically placed. (Someone actually told me to put out my worn underwear, but I didn't want it to look like a crime scene!) In order to put my smell in the vicinity, I rubbed dry dog food in my hands. Before I tossed it about, Linda Corson suggested I spit on it to really give it my scent. So I spat on it. I spat and spat on a bag of dry dog food until I dehydrated myself. Forty pounds of it spread amongst the bushes and cemetery. My mouth felt like the Sahara Desert. *This is sure to keep her here*, I thought.

We needed one more thing. The bait. I thought of foods with strong aromas that would allure Louise. Once, when I made pork and sauerkraut, Ray smelled the kraut all the way down in our family room. Then I remembered throwing away an empty can of tuna and the dogs upsetting the garbage can to retrieve it. I hadn't researched anything about dog traps, or if people had more success with dog food or anything else used as bait. Besides, Louise was not a picky eater. I decided to bring along the tuna. My hunch about the tuna's potent aroma proved right. Mr. Congenial Calico Cat was back in no time, intertwining my legs, sashaying the scene, and being his pesky self. He made a beeline for the trap. *Dang, I should have brought the sauerkraut*, I thought.

"This cat's got to go," I told Ginger.

"I can't take him," she said. "I have too many dogs at my house."

Speaking with a parched mouth, I called Shawna, our Furry Friends Network cat lady. With my last drop of saliva left in me, I told her I needed to remove this stray cat from the premises.

"Our foster homes are all full," she answered. "I have nowhere to house him."

"Please, Shawna," I begged. "He's interfering with Operation Louise. He'll be the one I catch in the trap. I can't take him home with me. My dogs will go nuts."

"I'll see what I can do and get back to you," she said.

This stray cat needed contained and out of the way. I decided to put him in a crate that I borrowed from Ginger, making sure he had food and water, of course. Choosing a shady place on the deck of the family home I was permitted to be trespassing on, I carried my unhappy hostage to his temporary holding cell. "This will be just for a little while," I told the kitty, "until we can find a foster home for you."

Ginger offered to keep an eye on the imprisoned cat and on the trap until I returned.

Next on my list that day was picking up Ranger, my former foster beagle. Everything came at me at once, it seemed. Apprehension haunted me about getting Ranger back. He had such a horrible adjustment to his new home when he first got adopted. He exhibited bad behaviors, such as chewing and mild separation anxiety, that I hadn't seen while he was in my foster care. I hoped I'd get my old Ranger back.

Ranger's owner met me at 1:00 p.m. There was my good old Ranger, a year later and a little chubbier. The man apologized for it not working out, gave me the dog's feeding dishes and supplies, and said a brief good-bye. Within five minutes, Ranger was my happy-go-lucky foster dog. My canine co-pilot tried to squeeze his plump belly between the steering wheel and me. Pants of warm doggy breath blew into my ear as he couldn't get close enough. Wet, slushy kisses pelted my cheeks. My lovable Ranger would have no trouble finding a new home. Ranger would be loved by his next forever family, I was sure. (Author note: Ranger was successfully adopted within a short period of time.)

Dropping Ranger off at my house, I let him get reacquainted with my dogs. Shawna phoned me at home with good news. A foster home opened up for the stray feline. She would come to pick up the cat in a few hours.

"This cat will really make a wonderful pet," I told her. "He's so affectionate you won't have any trouble adopting him out."

"I hope so," said Shawna. "Andrea has a litter of kittens at her house now. She really didn't want to take another cat. It took some convincing."

I thanked Shawna, telling her I owed her a huge favor and would somehow pay her back. Things were looking up. Ranger was glad to be on his own turf, and Furry Friends Network could help the new stray cat find a forever home. Now, all we needed was for the trap to work and Operation Louise to be a success. That last one was hoping with a leap of faith, I decided.

For the umpteenth time, I whisked over to Mechanicsburg. Even with Ginger checking the trap, I couldn't sit at home. She saw me walking around the pine trees and came over with something in her hand. It was some kind of instrument.

"Guess what I have?" she said in a sing-song voice.

"Well, it can't be Louise in your palm," I joked.

"I have a night vision monitor lens," she quipped.

"A *what?*" I asked, being technologically disadvantaged. I'm also computer illiterate. My media skills consisted of typing a parent newsletter with one finger and sending emails.

"We can attach it to a tree or fence and I'll be able to see what's going on in the trap from my house," Ginger answered.

"Wow," I said. "Operation Louise is going high tech!"

Everything was in place. The night lens was attached to a tree branch and aimed at the trap. The smell of tuna permeated the air. Strewn about were Louise's chew toys, rope toy, hooves, and oval pet bed. My filthy jeans, sweatshirt that reeked with my body odor, and grungy sneaker socks blanketed the area. Slightly moistened kibble dredged the ground near the trap's entrance.

The stage was set. All we could do was wait.

"There's nothing you can do here, Sharon," said Ginger. "Go home or get some errands done. I'll keep an eye on the trap," she offered.

"I suppose you're right," I answered. "I could use the time."

My Saturday slate of "Reminders to Do," which hung on the fridge, was as long as Santa's list. Overdue dry cleaning awaited pick up, a bank deposit was needed to cover bills, and my car's blinking oil light reminded me of my tardiness in getting the oil changed. Checking off my chores as I completed my tasks gave me a sense of satisfaction and took my mind, at least now and then, off of Operation Louise.

Later that evening, I patrolled the clock and held a vigil by the phone. Around 9:00 p.m., I couldn't stand it anymore. "I'm going over to drive around the area again," I said to Ray.

"Are you sure?" Ray asked. "The trap is there."

"She's out at night," I replied. It was my best chance to find Louise.

Back in Louise Land, I held the flashlight out my car window and inspected the cemetery grounds in the dark of the night. Nothing but tombstones overlooked the land. For two more hours, I traveled the same familiar paths, the same streets, the same neighborhoods. Looking, scanning, peering with my body hanging out of the car like I was attempting to grab the brass ring on a merry-go-round. *Please stay around the trap, Louise,* I thought. I drove so slowly on Wertzville Road that I was a hazard to other drivers. Upcoming cars in the rear approached too quickly. They were on my tail in no time as I put my eyes back on the road and cruised up to speed. Then I spied something behind the guardrail. I wasn't sure if it had white fur. It was hazy. I couldn't get a good look, it moved so quickly. For a second its eye reflected on my headlights and vanished. I slammed on my brakes, only to be honked at and cursed by the vehicle behind me. Without signaling, I turned the corner and parked the car. The flashlight beaconed into nothing but vines and undergrowth. Spotting a drainpipe, I was sure that would be the perfect place for her to hide. Slipping on shale, I trekked down a gully to the ridged culvert. The hollow cylinder answered me with echoed emptiness as I summoned for Louise. If it was her I spotted, she was gone. I clambered back up to the car.

By now, it was getting late. The past few nights of my midnight madness caught up with me. With the car parked and my head propped against the steering wheel, I sobbed as exhaustion overcame me. Driving home, I fought to stay awake as my eyes half closed. I blared the car radio to stay focused, tuning into an "Oldies but Goodies" station so I could sing along to keep me awake. With squinted eyes, I concentrated on the white lines on the road and sang the Bee Gees', *Stayin' Alive,* in my loudest off-key vocals.

It had been a challenging day. The trap, the stray cat, Ranger. I was emotionally drained. Ray waited up for me as I plopped on the couch.

"I think I saw her again tonight, but I'm not certain," I told him. "Ray, I don't think I can do this anymore," I said. "I can't go on like this. I can't take anymore. If the trap doesn't work, I'm done." That night was the lowest of the lows. Perhaps it was time to let go.

"What? Are you crazy?" shouted Ray. He glared at me from the recliner. "We're this close to catching her," he said, gesturing an inch measurement with his index finger and thumb. "We're not giving up the ship now!"

Ray tucked me in bed and attributed my mental breakdown to being delirious from fatigue. Ray was my anchor in the storm. "There's always tomorrow," he said gently.

The next morning I awoke about 6:30 a.m. with a heavy heart. Getting out of bed was a chore since it wasn't a school day. I couldn't face another day of searching, another day without Louise. What must have been clinical depression ate at my soul. The desire to get a shower or get dressed was stifled. My dirty blond, uncombed, greasy hair seemed irrelevant. That first cup of coffee didn't hit the spot. Deciding what to defrost for Sunday dinner, or even eating for that matter, seemed unimportant. The dogs looked at me with their "go get the leash" faces, but I turned away, whereas, we were normally out the door by quarter to seven sharp. I'd only been up a short while, but time passed in slow motion. Perhaps it was my bleak outlook that made minutes drag like hours.

At 7:00 a.m., the phone rang. Although quite early in the morning on a Sunday, I didn't think much of it because Ray and our daughter, Alicia, had plans to go to a newly opened flea market. They had arranged to meet for breakfast first. Expecting it was her, Ray answered the phone, but handed it to me. I looked at him puzzled. "Is something wrong?" I asked. "Is my mom sick?" Anxiety pervaded me as I braced myself for bad news.

"Sharon, you'd better get over here. Your dog is barking up a storm," Ginger announced excitedly. "She sure has a set of lungs on her!" Thinking the unforeseen call was from a family member, it took me a minute to realize it was Ginger. My incredible Louise tried to bark her way out of the trap, waking up the whole neighborhood!

My knees wobbled, gave out from under me, and hit the kitchen floor with a thud. Cries, screams, laughter, and hysterics erupted from me all at once. Tears flooded my face as I choked on my words trying to respond to Ginger. A medley of feelings – joy, relief, excitement, and disbelief - surged from my soul. Rising to my feet, I jumped up and down hollering in garbled speech, "It worked! We have her!" Ray looked at me as though I had escaped from the lunatic asylum. All along Ray imploded his feelings. I made up for the both of us as three weeks of bottled up emotions shot out of me like a cannon. I grabbed my car keys and dashed out the door.

"Wait a minute! You can't go like that," Ray insisted. In my state of mania, I ran across the yard to our truck in my nightgown.

"Oops, you're right," I said to Ray as I backtracked and quickly threw on sweat clothes.

"I'll drive separately and see you over there," Ray said, still wanting to meet Alicia later at the restaurant.

Gunning my family-sized sedan, I made the normal twenty-five minute trip to Mechanicsburg in twelve minutes flat. My seat belt clasp couldn't unbuckle fast enough as I slammed the car into park. Due to my white-knuckled driving, I fumbled removing my keys from the ignition. My legs couldn't run fast enough to the trap. There she was, hunched over, tail down, white fur streaked with brown mud, her tell-tale white splotched ear marking, making her unmistakably Louise. Her trembling body rattled the cage. An empty food dish inside the trap was tongued shiny and clean.

My Louise stood right there in the trap before my eyes. For all the grief she put me through, I didn't know whether to hug her or shake her. When I approached, Louise wagged her tail. "That's the first she's done that," Ginger said to me. Louise wiggled with delight when she spotted me. With misty eyes, I ran to my little darling. But something repulsed me as I drew near. That wasn't brown mud on her fur. I don't know what on earth that stuff is that dogs roll in, but Louise had smeared herself in it. It was the most rancid stench I ever whiffed. I didn't care. My Louise was back! And I embraced her, raunchy smell and all, through the steel bars. She licked my face as though it was a lollipop. I kissed her snout a hundred times through the cage, not wanting to know what she had her mouth on in the past three weeks. Ray observed our reunion from the sidelines while dry heaving and gagging from the putrid smell coming from Louise. Despite the odor, Ray was also excited that we had finally found our malodorous little girl.

Ginger witnessed the bond between Louise and me and commented, "I can't believe how much she loves you, Sharon."

"That's our Louise! She can be almost normal with me," I replied.

Still in shock that the trap worked the first night, the three of us, Ray, Ginger, and I, began to behold our canine catch in silence. Saying nothing said everything. We stood in ineffable bliss for a few moments, gazing at Louise with reverence. Ginger and I cried and hugged. We shared stories of special needs fosters, which bonded our newly formed friendship. We parted, ecstatic on a job well done. We in rescue know there's nothing like a happy ending. We hoped our paths would cross again, but in happier circumstances, and not by an escaped, scared dog.

Not risking taking Louise out of the trap, I carried the pungent prisoner to my car. Ray gathered up the conglomeration of doggy collectibles and my clothes and pitched them in my trunk. Spinning my tires on the gravel road, I bid farewell to the cemetery. *No more driving past tombstones tonight or any night, no more pilgrimages to Mechanicsburg*, I thought, as I covered my hand over my nose and mouth to simulate a gas mask. Louise zonked out in the trap in the backseat on the ride back to Dauphin. Nose tucked under her paws, the sound of her muffled snores competed with the radio. "We're home now," I told my little princess.

Once inside, I carried Louise at arm's length straight up to the bathtub. Streams of brown, cruddy water swirled in the drain as I drenched herbal scented shampoo on her filthy fur. I swabbed cotton balls of dark wax and crusty scabs out of her ears. Blood engorged ticks polluted her body as I pulled out chunks of skin while they clung to their last meal. *Die, you nasty parasites*, I thought, as they plunged to their death in a container of cooking oil.

Cleaned and conditioned after her makeover, Louise was as white as bleached linens. She returned with a voracious appetite, inhaling a bowl of food like she hadn't eaten in three weeks. Well, she probably hadn't, I reasoned. With a full belly, she snuggled in her pet bed and soon fell asleep. Exhausted from her escapade, she snoozed all day. I did little else but watch and adore her, as she was curled in her cocoon. My imagination exploded, I could only surmise the enterprises and obstacles she must have encountered while loose. Too bad I couldn't have been a tick and gone along for the ride. I was getting silly in my excitement of Louise being home.

Reality as well as relief set in once again. It was a blessing for Louise to be in one piece. Other than tons of ticks, she was unscathed. She never got hit by a car, eaten by a coyote, or badly scraped while prodding through all those brambles. She appeared to be in good shape, although much skinnier. She'd put some weight on those bony ribs in no time. Health-wise, Louise beat the odds. But then a consideration disturbed my upbeat celebratory thoughts. What if we had to start at the beginning with her rehabilitation?

What if Louise regressed where she wouldn't like the walks again or let Ray leash her? Did she need housetrained all over again? Would Louise remember her life here with us or did she return to us a feral dog?

My questions were answered when Ray walked in the door. Louise greeted him like a child running to open their presents on Christmas morning. Nothing had changed. Although she was still our neurotic Louise, she didn't seem traumatized by her escape. She curled up on the couch with me, tossed some doggy toys about, and had no potty accidents in the house that day. She acted like she never left us.

Needing to thank everyone who was involved in her safe return, Robin sent a mass email to all the rescues indicating Louise was home. Messages saying, "Way to go" and "I knew you'd get her back" overflowed my inbox. Fellow rescuers celebrated with me. They sent their heartfelt congratulations. Neighbors and friends were amazed at the determination and drastic measures Ray and I took to get Louise back.

"I would have given up in a couple days," admitted Ray's closest buddy. "You have the patience of a saint."

"How did you work full time and do all that driving around?" asked another teacher.

"You sat in a cemetery?" said a Furry Friends Network acquaintance. These were some of the favorable responses we received. The vast majority of comments were positive, but there are always a few skeptics in the crowd.

One man emailed me during her absence and made it very clear that I should not have interfered with Louise's freedom. He imagined Louise was born an undomesticated pack dog running amuck in the foothills of West Virginia. It was best to leave well enough alone. Humans stick them in crates, hampering the way nature meant it to be. Louise was happier in the wild, he thought. Let her go, he demanded.

Another lady, obviously not a canine lover, remarked acridly to me, "She's not even your dog. You'd think you lost a child."

"I did," I replied.

Beagle Bit

Dogs with droopy, hanging ears are vulnerable to ear (both yeast and bacterial) infections. Air cannot circulate and dry out the ear as easily in floppy-eared dogs. Watch for shaking of the head, scratching, unpleasant odor, increased wax, and redness. Along with hearing, a dog's ears give it a sense of balance.

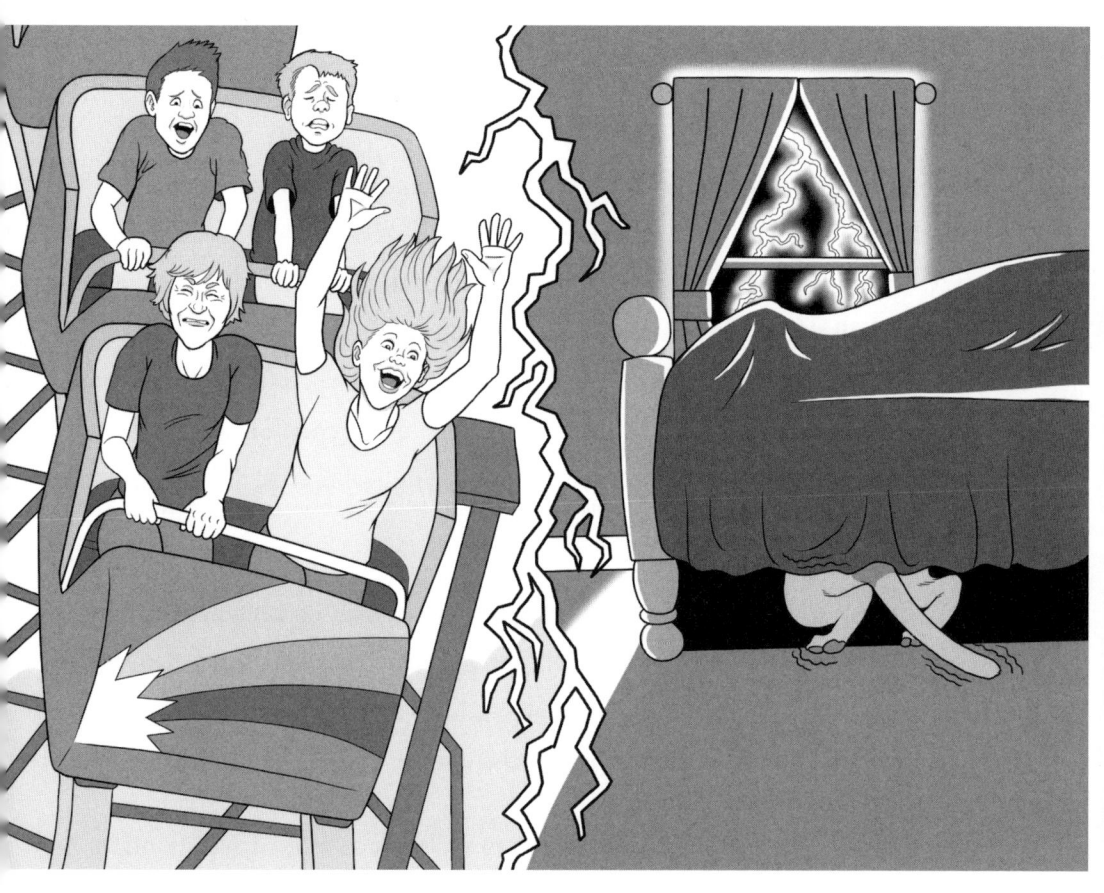

Chapter Fourteen

Big Booms Home and Away

My jaws never stopped flapping that Monday morning of May 1. Did I ever have a story to tell my students! Like a Girl Scout sitting around a campfire, I reiterated my weekend of Louise's incredible capture. I spouted details of zombies that arose from the dead at night in the cemetery, a crazy calico cat that was a stray and then got rescued, and my stinky Louise home safe and sound.

The students marveled at my antics. Some met me with strange stares as they probably felt their teacher was a bit mentally imbalanced for the time I spent in a cemetery, especially late at night. They shouted peals of laughter when Ray gagged from the reeking smell of our captive canine. They cheered with glee and applauded that I caught Louise. They gasped sighs of pity when I recounted the painful extraction of the ticks all over Louise's body. No one loved telling this experience, or hearing it, more than I did! I could tell it a hundred times and I would not get tired of it. My Louise was no longer on the lam…she was home!

Later in the day, one student occupied herself writing run-on sentences in a spiral theme notebook. The graphite of her well-chewed pencil stroked and balanced the lined paper. She concealed her fervent scribbling halfway in her desk during the math lesson. She stopped only to shake out her hand cramps.

"What are you working on?" I asked, ready to scold her for not paying attention.

"I'm writing an animal story," she replied. "I want to rescue dogs like you do when I grow up. Mrs. Cree, you ought'a write a book about Louise!"

"I just might do that someday," I told this precocious child.

With Louise back at home, life assumed its normal routines and the warm, spring days rolled on. My everyday habits of walking the beagles, maintaining a big house, yard work, concocting a suitable supper, working with Louise's phobias and fears of noise and people, and doing mounds of schoolwork fell back into track. But teaching school in May and finishing the year was difficult, even for a veteran teacher. Spring fever, or what I term, "May-itis," hit third graders like an epidemic of chicken pox. Ball games, hiking, and playing outside on the jungle gym took precedence over doing homework. Isn't riding a bike on a warm spring evening better than staying inside reciting spelling words? Who feels like memorizing vocabulary words for science when it's more fun to go to the playground and swing?

Mentally, academics exasperated the kids. They knew that by May, they wouldn't "flunk" or have to repeat third grade with three semesters of passing grades under their belts. What's the sense of studying times tables in May when you'd forget them over the summer, anyway? Seven hours a day cooped up in one room with the same classmates since August took its toll. The children were uncooperative and picked on each other. Tempers flared as complaints of, "he gypped me," "she won't take turns," or "he won't let me be on his kickball team," heightened. They tattled at the slightest infraction. Still drained from the tumultuous three weeks Louise was missing, my energy needed revamping. Everyone anticipated the arrival of summer, no one more than I.

On June 9, group hugs were the order. The last day of school was in session. My class watched a movie as room parents trickled in with goodies for our end of the year party. Children roamed to one another requesting signatures in their autograph books. Posters of "My Summer Vacation Plans" were the Show and Tell for the day. Collecting textbooks and cleaning out cubbies got the kids fired up. One student finally found an undone homework paper, which he previously had profusely proclaimed his dog ate. Bouquets of flowers from well-wishing parents and handfuls of dandelions from the kids covered my lesson plans on top of my desk. Anxious to see their fourth grade room assignment, they tore open their report cards like they were envelopes at the

Academy Awards. Yellow buses honked their horns as they circled the designated pick up area one last time at dismissal. *I hope I made a difference in their lives this school year,* I thought after the students left for their summer vacation. Before I left for my own summer vacation, I scrubbed crayon marks off desktops in my vacant classroom.

That night my daughter Jessica called me.

"Mom, summer's here. You never come to see me. You always put those dogs first," she scolded me.

"You're right," I told her. "You have every reason to complain. I promised you I'd come to visit you and never did."

Three years prior to this, Jessica accepted a college internship at a theme park in Orlando, Florida. She applied in November of 2003 and got the exciting news over Christmas break that she'd been hired for a five-month internship term. Apprehensive about living in another state, she was unsure about being so far from home. She currently was attending Shippensburg University, which was only about an hour from us. If sickness struck or an emergency arose, she was still close enough to rely on our help. Working for this major theme park, the opportunity of a lifetime awaited her. This experience would look good on her resume. Who could decline living in a warmer climate? "Do it while you're young," I told her. "You'd be crazy to pass up an opportunity like this."

So, we packed up her red 1999 sports car, leaving only peek holes to see the traffic out the rear view mirror. With her heaps of clothes, shoes, toiletries, a small TV, linens, and lamps, we resembled the *Beverly Hillbillies* loading up their jalopy moving to California.

Only we were heading to Florida, one thousand miles away. The sixteen-hour road trip, although cramped, gave mother and daughter a chance to bond. It was bittersweet. With this trip, my child was leaving the nest to spread her wings.

Jessica's temporary internship turned permanent. She remained in Orlando for the next three years, flying home to see us only at Christmastime. She called numerous times asking me to fly down for a visit, offering that she had complimentary tickets to the theme parks. I was always too busy. Tired of my excuses that I couldn't leave the dogs or had too many fosters, she felt abandoned. Ashamed I did not treat her as a priority, I decided to visit later that month. I owed my daughter that much. Besides, I deserved it after Louise's venture. How could I pass up an adventurous one-week vacation in Florida with my daughter?

Palm trees, swimming pools, sandy beaches, and dog-less days of summer looked inviting. *An excursion will do me good,* I thought. I can sleep in past 6:00 a.m. No barking for seven whole days. Wouldn't it be great to get a break from vacuuming dog hair and cleaning up dog droppings several times a day? Dogs in, dogs out. All I did was take care of dogs. Whose turn is it to go out? Who is due for their heartworm preventative? What dog chewed my sneaker? Who puked on the loveseat? Who needs their nails clipped? Although I was not complaining, the work was never ending.

Speaking of those clippers (click, click), now all I had to do was figure out what to do with Louise while I was gone. This would be the first time I was away from her. (Well, other than the three weeks when Louise was on the lam.) We wouldn't consider putting her in a kennel. There was no need to board her since Ray would still be home. The biggest hurdle was how to cope with her frequent peeing during the day while he worked twelve-hour days. A urine sample checked by our vet revealed no infections. An ultrasound on her bladder showed no imperfections. Louise simply peed a lot because of her bad nerves. The medication the vet prescribed for anxiety the day of her escape had not decreased her peeing. The pet door was not an option since the slapping of its flap scared her. To ease the situation, Ray promised to leave a little later in the morning and hurry home each evening. But Louise still needed to go out during the day.

To deal with our dog dilemma, I sought the help of Stephanie Grossnickle, another Furry Friends Network volunteer. Stephanie agreed to come to my house twice a day, morning and afternoon. We are the best of friends. Stephanie is a dear woman and a kind soul. She is the type of person who says, "God Bless You" in everyday conversation or apologizes when things aren't even her fault. She has a gentle demeanor and the patience to deal with Louise, a perfect candidate with her nurturing manner. We scheduled Stephanie to meet Louise prior to my trip.

Louise's avoidance of Stephanie amazed her. Dogs can usually sense that a person is a "dog person" and have no qualms greeting a rescuer. People with an aura, like Stephanie, who send vibrations of calmness and love, are naturally welcomed by canines. Not Louise. It was another human, of course. Stephanie stooped down and tried to attract Louise to her, coaxing her with soft words and nonthreatening body gestures. Slow moves, no eye contact, and the "let her come to me" options also proved unsuccessful. Louise paced in circles, evading Stephanie, wanting nothing to do with this outsider.

Stephanie knew how much this trip meant to me. She sympathized all too well with the day-to-day work of taking care of so many dogs and the anguish I suffered when Louise was missing. She also had a grown son who lived out of state and she encouraged me to spend time with my daughter.

"Go enjoy yourself, Sharon," she told me. "If worse comes to worse, I'll catch her by luring her with treats."

"Or maybe she'll be so scared of you, she'll run out the pet door to get away," I half-joked.

With thorough travel plans orchestrated, I covered every detail of my absence, thinking with Ray and Stephanie's help, Louise now had several opportunities to eliminate throughout the day. That took care of Louise's biggest issue. But I didn't stop there. I organized and wrote specific directions about the dogs' medicines, feedings, and walk schedules. Cans of dog food, biscuits, and rawhide sticks sat in plain view for Ray on the kitchen counter. The regular vet number, an emergency animal clinic, Stephanie's cell, and my flight timetable hung from a beagle magnet near the phone. Like an old mother hen, I lectured poor Ray with condescending instructions.

"Make sure you put Louise out to potty first thing in the morning. You have to watch her. If she doesn't potty, put her out again before you leave," I reminded Ray.

"Yeah, yeah," he retorted. "I haven't exactly been hiding in a cave. I live here too, you know. Go and have a good time and quit worrying."

To be extra cautious, I placed plastic drop cloths, blankets, and comforters on our living room wall-to-wall carpets in case Louise had accidents. We had tried doggy diapers at one time, but she ripped them to shreds. Penning her in the kitchen on the linoleum floor didn't work. She jumped the baby gate and flew over it like the cow jumped over the moon. Louise hated any type of confinement. And since she loathed the crate, I thought it best to leave her loose in the house. She didn't need silver teeth again from gnawing the bars of the cage. Louise stressed from anything out of the ordinary. She was accustomed to remaining loose and non-contained in the house. Besides, I'd only be gone for a week. What could go wrong? I assured myself. My shoulders drooped as I thought, *Anything can go wrong if it's Louise!*

I booked an inexpensive direct flight to Florida leaving from Baltimore. It was only an hour and a half drive from our home and saved me a lot of money, compared to leaving from the closer Harrisburg International Airport. The morning of my departure was crisp and clear. My sneakers dampened with dew from the grass while loading my suitcases in the car. I gave Louise an extra hug, telling her to be a good girl for Daddy. The dogs watched me from the bay window as I backed out the driveway. The looks on their faces said, "Mommy's just going to the grocery store. She'll be back in a little while." The other beagles would be fine, I knew, but I felt guilty for leaving Louise. At least, I figured, she'd enjoy the comforts of home. I reminded myself that I was due for a vacation after all that Louise had put me through. And, I was looking forward to spending time with my daughter, Jessica, too, in the heart of the entertainment universe, Orlando, Florida!

A smooth flight and no layovers to contend with ushered in the start of a great getaway. The aerial patchwork view of Pennsylvania's fertile farmland soon turned into the alligator infested wetlands of Florida. My daughter's face beamed with delight when she spotted me walking down the airport tunnel. There was Jessica, bronzed skin and sun- bleached hair, looking like a true resident of the Sunshine State. *I should have done this sooner,* I thought.

After unpacking, we hung out together and postponed the big attractions until the next day. We relaxed by the pool as palm trees swayed in warm, balmy breezes. A sudden thunderstorm sent us scrambling inside for the rest of the afternoon. By suppertime, I was starving. My stomach had long since digested my hearty meal of three peanuts on the airplane. Jessica, a single, working girl who lacked cooking skills, had little interest in preparing gourmet foods or meals of any kind. Each of her roommates had an allotted shelf in the refrigerator filled with groceries, but Jessica's space was bare. Cans of spaghetti and quick cooking noodle packages were stockpiled in the cupboards by the other tenants, but Jessica's space could have been occupied by Old Mother Hubbard. So, Mom paid for a nice dinner out.

Then we shopped at designer outlets the rest of the evening. Jessica needed some dress pants for work. We lugged our purchases back to the car as the store lights dimmed. Sales associates pulled security gates down over the thresholds and hung "Closed" signs on the doors. On the drive home, I saw every out-of-state license plate except Alaska and Hawaii.

At 10:00 p.m., during our profound mother daughter conversation about boyfriends and adulthood, the house shook like an earthquake hit. Living room windows rattled and jarred. A wham-bam sounded like a dresser fell over upstairs. I could have sworn a car backfired in her bathroom.

"What was *that*?" I asked, ready to dive underneath the coffee table.

"Oh, that happens every night. You'll learn to ignore it," she said. "Those are the fireworks at the theme park. We can see them in the backyard. Better get a good night's sleep because we have a big day planned for tomorrow!"

New adventures awaited me! The inviting motto above the entrance sign to the theme park welcomed us. We arrived when the doors opened and parked what seemed like four miles from the main gate. Our ride on the tram was motion enough for me and the gentle breeze felt good as we passed row after row of cars. Having prepurchased tickets enabled us to gain access into the park quickly without having to wait in lines.

"Is this what it's like to be a tourist?" I asked Jessica as perspiration dripped down my forehead. "How do you breathe in this heat?"

"You'll get used to the humidity," she said. "Isn't this fun, Mom?"

The temperature soared into the nineties plus add to that the high humidity. A sunny-side-up egg could have fried on my head. Each ride or show had a minimum forty-five minute waiting period. My legs ached as I stood with a robust, burly man who reeked of tobacco and breathed down my neck. Never had I seen so many people crammed into one place. A cranky toddler that needed a nap, whining and fussing, was always behind me in line. A two year old, throwing a temper tantrum that he wanted another cotton candy, always managed to be in front of me.

Despite the oodles of people and scorching heat, the vacation recharged my verve. The teacher in me loved journeying through the eleven different country pavilions. Each building offered culture, architecture, music, décor, clothing, and restaurants indicative of the customs of that country. We entered Mexico through a model of an Aztec pyramid. We ate our way through the international foods as I purchased baskets, pottery, and souvenir attire. A sombrero and poncho would complete my teaching unit on south of the border. The conservationist in me wanted to have a look inside the environmental pavilion. We boarded a boat ride and learned that plants hooked up to

IVs could thrive without soil. I'd have to revise my third grade lecture that plants do not need dirt and introduce hydroponics. We had the most fun in the theater with the 3D show. I always wondered what function those funny glasses served. A hose jumped out of the screen and squirted us. Later in the movie, when a viper opened its mouth dislodging its jaws like a bear trap, I thought I was going to get eaten alive!

Another day we visited another part of the theme park. Jessica suggested we get cooled off on a water flume ride. She insisted on sitting at the front of the flume. My stomach came up to my throat as we plunged fifty-two and one-half feet. It wasn't a splash. It was more of a tidal wave that drenched us. Squish, squish went my tennis shoes the rest of the day. Daredevil Jessica coerced me to try another coaster ride assuring me I would not get wet. I should have paid attention to all the warnings advising against the ride if you have back problems, are pregnant, or have heart trouble. None of these categories pertained to me, so I thought I was safe. The notice should have also stated, "If you are a scaredy-cat, don't ride this ride." Even though the sixty-miles-per-hour rocket ride was in the dark, I closed my eyes anyway and screamed bloody murder. At least the sharp turns and sudden drops were over in two and one-half minutes. My hands were in a locked position from holding onto the front safety bar in a death grip. After I unkinked my fingers, I figured a more suitable ride would be the teacups. *These are a cinch to handle,* I thought. Jessica controlled the steering wheel as if she were captain at the helm. Maintaining the maximum rotation, our giant teacup whirled 360s nonstop. My head spun like a pinwheel!

With our hopper passes, we could go back and forth to several parks in one day. At one of the theme parks, I wouldn't dare step foot in a tall tower that dropped guests in a kind of cage straight down from a very high platform. My thrill seeker daughter shrieked as she plummeted thirteen stories down an elevator shaft in a matter of seconds. Hearing the patrons cry, "Oh my gosh!" or "Get me off!" I was happy to be an onlooker.

"That was wild!" exclaimed Jessica as she exited the attraction, ready to re-enter the entrance line.

"How about if we see a children's show next?" I pleaded. "You didn't inherit your dauntless courage from me."

So we compromised and visited the water parks. Jessica and I are both sun worshippers. I felt like I was in the Atlantic Ocean, only cleaner, as a wave slammed me in the expansive pool at one of the water parks. At another water park, I glided down a high-speed water slide as steep as a ski slope. At the finish line, my bathing suit bottom was up to my neck. Sprawled on my inner tube, I drifted down a smooth flowing waterway. *This is more my style*, I thought as I circled around and around the slow flowing stream like a lazy Susan. No fright, no flight, the ultimate in relaxation. But after an hour of leisure floating, my white legs turned lobster red as the intense sun baked me like a burnt cookie.

Despite the massive crowds, the stinging of my scarlet limbs, and Mom's party-pooper ways, the vacation did me good. A feeling of being a kid again came over me as I watched the parade with its dazzling lights and a cast of characters stroll down the street. As the attractions glistened in the background, costumed characters waved from their floats in this illuminated nighttime procession. The fun-filled parks were a sharp contrast to my simple and content country life in Dauphin.

Compared to my role of a housewife, teacher and foster mom to beagles, Jessica's daily routine was entirely different. When I was her age, I was already married, teaching elementary school full time, and raising her. I never experienced a carefree time in college or a party hardy existence. Now, in her early twenties, she possessed a good work ethic like her mom, but was able to come and go as she pleased. There were no pets in the household and no one to answer to. Forking over her share of the rent each month was her biggest concern, but she had no husband, child, or family responsibilities. Her major decision each morning was what to wear to work, and at night, where to bar hop. She'd tell her roommates, "See ya," in the morning and head out the door. I was glad to see the girls got along. They became as close as sisters. They borrowed each other's new shirt or curling iron, but never sat down to a meal together. Everyone got up, got dressed, and ran out the door to their jobs. When they got home, they changed clothing and went off again. It wasn't a home; it was a dorm. The entrance to the house was a revolving door with friends and other interns in and out. It was customary to leave at 10:00 p.m. to see a movie or comedy show. Back at home, that was my bedtime. The only thing that resembled a homestead in their apartment was a job chart on the refrigerator. Jessica confessed no one performed their chores or they'd check off their name and not accomplish the task anyway. When I arrived, the stained toilet, dried crumbs on countertops, dusty end tables, and cobwebs looked like no one cleaned in months. Who wants to clean when you're having so much fun? Every hour was happy hour. *Oh, to be young and carefree*, I thought.

We toured the attractions from opening until closing the next several days, sometimes arriving home after midnight. I kept up with the youthful ones staying up so late. We were the "girls on the go," as opposed to my sitting on the couch and watching television most evenings in Pennsylvania. But by mid-week, I caught a glimpse of the national news as we stayed in one evening and prepared a home-cooked dinner. Weathermen reported widespread flooding and torrential rains in the northeast. Rivers crested, people evacuated their homes, and waterlogged businesses sat in ruins. Sand bags prevented further damage in some towns able to prepare for the disaster. Rescue boats saved stranded residents standing on rooftops.

Fearing our area was affected, I called Ray to ask about the status of the Susquehanna River. Harrisburg sits along the banks of this non-navigable waterway. Before I left, Ray made me promise to enjoy myself, forget about the dogs for a week, and stop fretting over Louise. Initially, I called him when I arrived in Florida to let him know I had a safe flight. He assured me everything was fine and that he'd phone if anything went wrong. He gave me strict orders not to pester him.

"Ray, I just saw the news. We've been running from morning until night. Are you okay?" I queried.

"We've had a lot of rain here. Terrible thunderstorms. The front yard is a big puddle," he replied. "The dogs have that wet, doggy smell all the time from going in and out in the pouring down rain. I'd rather sniff a pile of musty, damp beach towels."

"Is Louise scared? How is she doing for you? Has Stephanie been coming in?" I asked while mashing potatoes.

"Are you having a good time down there?" Ray asked, trying to get my mind off the floods.

"Yes, it's a far cry from Dauphin. We can see the fireworks from Jessica's porch every night. The whole house shakes. So, is Stephanie coming twice a day?" I asked again.

"How does Jessica like her job? Did you meet her roommates?" Ray questioned.

"She loves her job. Her roommates are fun to be with. One works at one theme park. Another one manages a store at another theme park. I don't see them much, but they're nice girls. So how's Louise?" I asked.

"I have everything under control. You enjoy the rest of your vacation and I'll see you when you get home. Bye," Ray answered. With that, he hung up.

"Ray kind of cut me off short," I said to Jessica, as I set the table. "I didn't get a chance to remind him to put Louise's specially designed jacket for wearing in thunderstorms on her."

"Oh, Mom, he never was much of a talker. Stop being a worrywart. Relax and have this glass of wine I poured you," Jessica told me as she stuffed an empty wine bottle into the already overflowing trash can. "Wow, a sit-down meal with homemade gravy. Let's eat! He's a big boy. He won't let anything happen to the dogs. Try not to think about them. We only have three more days left."

She was right. The dogs were in good hands. I was here to enjoy my time with my daughter.

We spent the latter part of the week visiting surrounding attractions outside the main theme parks in Orlando. At one park, alligators leaped for raw chicken meat and rolled in a frenzy to ingest it. These reptiles didn't bother me as long as I knew they were contained, but if I saw one in Jessica's backyard I'd probably faint. We both love dolphins, so we had to visit the theme park that featured them. Killer whales sprayed us as they waved their flippers, jumped through hoops of fire, and took the trainer for a piggyback ride. The animal lover in me thought the show using pets in amusing activities and antics, was just about the cutest thing. Rescued animals, everything from dogs, cats, birds, and a pot-bellied pig, performed comical tricks and skits. "Hooray for rescue!" I shouted at the end of the performance. While we waited for a pirate show featuring sea lions and a walrus to begin, a mime imitated people in the audience. With his painted white face, he poked fun at people as they took their seats. Jessica and I almost fell off our bleacher laughing as he copied a pregnant lady's waddle, a youngster throwing his pacifier, and a man with a beer belly who couldn't find his wife. We joked that he was funnier than the show.

The nightlife, the sun, the attractions, even the house sounding like a train barreled through it at 10:00 p.m. - I was evolving into a Floridian. But alas, my vacation was coming to an end. Time to head back to reality. My heart sank as I said good-bye to Jessica at the airport. It would be months until we saw each other again, but I was only a phone call away. I was proud that I raised an independent, responsible young lady who was making her way in the world. And, what a great place to plant her future.

Back at the Baltimore airport in early afternoon, the television monitors revealed serious devastation from the pounding rains. Downpours plagued the Mid-Atlantic states all week. Traffic halted in some parts of Baltimore as water rose to dangerous levels on expressways. Mass flooding hit vast areas, not just regional creeks and streams. Unnerved by these reports, I felt fortunate that my drive home was not affected. To my relief, it was smooth sailing straight up Interstate 83 across state lines from Baltimore to my home in Dauphin, Pennsylvania. Anxious to get home and survey our local damage, I resisted the temptation to stop at my favorite shopping center in York, Pennsylvania, on the way back.

Fluorescent orange detour signs blocked one of the roads to my neighborhood. I avoided branches and tree limbs that littered the ground as I rerouted my travel. Debris, washed down by rushing streams, cluttered the countryside. Brown, muddy water from Clark's Creek spilled over the pavement flooding nearby fields and gardens. Neighbors in hip waders photographed the deluge. Some dare devils drove through impassable streets as their cars splashed through fender high puddles.

When I finally arrived home, I could see that my front yard looked like a swamp. Normally in June we took pride in our well-manicured, green velvet lawn. When I left for Florida, my red geraniums and pink petunias were in full bloom. Now, the saturated grass was barely visible through nature's murky pool. The flowers, battered by heavy showers, drooped their weakened stems. Small shrubs and azaleas looked as if they'd been trampled by cattle. Pelting rains dragged tanbark down our sidewalk. Mother Nature carried limestone rocks from our neighbor's unpaved driveway onto our property.

I pulled into the garage anxious to unload my suitcase from the trunk. Water gushed from the car tires and left liquid patties on the cement floor. Slushing through small puddles, I finally retrieved my luggage. When I slammed the trunk closed, my canine family was alerted to my return. I'd forgotten how loud the beagles' bellowing really was. Plugging my ears, I stepped into the kitchen. Riley charged me like a linebacker, knocking me down. BuddyLee, postured like a coyote, serenaded me in his chorus of howls. And Louise gyrated her little rump when she reunited with her mommy, licking me like I was a big slab of juicy steak.

After surviving the beagle besiege, I passed the pile of unopened junk mail on the dining room table and ambled into the living room. A worn out, burgundy blanket with its torn satin border replaced the faded, blue flowered quilt I had spread on the floor before I left. Instead of the striped beach towel with frayed edges lying in the hallway, two white bath towels with yellow stains appeared in its place. Unfamiliar old sheets and comforters, hidden in the bottom of our bathroom closet along with the dust balls, now lined the family room. The fragrant smell of dryer sheets drew me to our adjacent laundry room. Lifting the washer lid, I discovered a spun dry load of towels awaiting removal. Lilac-scented blankets tumbled out of the dryer as I opened its door. Two puddles of urine dispersed on the vinyl floor right underneath the doggy door. As I staged my movements to avoid Louise's piddles, I realized the front yard wasn't the only place where a flood struck. In disbelief, I counted nine fresh deposits of Little Miss Pee Pot. I gathered up the freshly soiled coverings to make yet another load for the washer.

Sitting on my suitcase, I reconnoitered the interior damage to our home. I didn't know we owned so many blankets and towels. Unable to fathom how everything had gone so wrong, I felt defeated and disillusioned. *I can't even go away*, I thought. In spite of all my careful efforts, my beagle planning was bootless. Didn't Stephanie make it up to the house? What on earth went on with Louise?

Calling Ray to let him know I was home, I inquired about his week of dog duty. I stifled my urge to interrogate him, not wanting to insult his ability of canine care.

Sounding innocently perplexed I asked, "What happened here?"

"Well, I didn't want to ruin your trip," Ray admitted. "I'm so glad you're home. It was awful. I had a heck of a time with Louise."

Ray confessed the harrowing ordeal of the past week. Severe thunderstorms afflicted central Pennsylvania and continued for days. Nature's fury was relentless. Riley and BuddyLee, not usually affected by weather's ravage, had to be dragged out to go potty in the drenching rain. They couldn't find the right spot to tinkle as their paws sunk in the mire. Ray protected them with a big black umbrella as gale force gusts almost blew him away like a vision of Mary Poppins. Good thing Ray's a big guy! Riley reacted to the harsh weather by emitting nervous, unceasing flatulence in the house for Ray's breathing enjoyment. BuddyLee, who often slept downstairs in the recliner like a lone wolf, crawled under the sheets with Ray every night. Louise was in a constant state of agitation as she trembled and paced from her brontophobia, fear of thunder, that causes anxiety. She refused to eat. She couldn't get settled each evening as flashes of lightning streaked through the windows. After hearing each boom of thunder, Louise vaulted off the mattress several times each night. Ray didn't know what kept him awake more, the flashes of lightning or Louise's panting as she hid under the bed.

That was only the beginning. One night Ray got up to use the bathroom. He stepped on a pile, or should I say a "surprise," left by one of the dogs, on the bedroom carpet. It gushed through his toes as he walked heels up to the toilet. Ray, unable to tolerate ghastly smells, gulped a slug of stomach medicine as he disinfected his foul foot. Every day, he came home to more yellow secretions on the linens. He said he's never done so much laundry in his life, having to borrow detergent from our neighbor. Three days after I left, he had already washed six loads of towels.

To make matters worse, Stephanie had a difficult time just getting to our home. "Road Closed" signs confronted her, making her reroute her travel on unfamiliar streets to reach our home. She couldn't catch the already frightened Louise. One day she sat on the couch a long time, calm and quiet. But as soon as she moved an inch, Louise took off running. She was unsuccessful at getting Louise to go potty in the stormy weather.

For the first time, Ray confessed he'd had it with Louise. It was the worst week ever. The man, who was my Rock of Gibraltar during Louise's escape, was at the end of his rope.

A few days later when things calmed down, I spoke with Linda Corson, who lent me the trap that caught Louise. Her insightfulness in dog dealings and expertise impressed me. I reasoned that Louise's prominent peeing was due to her intense fear of thunderstorms. But I am not keen on all canine behaviors. Linda's take on our horrible week had a new twist. Linda felt that Louise may have thought that I was lost. Since dogs explore their world by their sense of smell, Louise urinated to leave her scent behind for me. Perhaps then I'd be able to find her. When hearing that, Ray and I couldn't be mad at our Louise. Understanding is the key to accepting a dog's shortcomings. Most people say their dog has a mind of its own.

With Louise, we were still trying to unlock the mysteries of her mind.

Beagle Bit

Charles Darwin's exploring ship was named the Beagle.

Chapter Fifteen

Aloha Louise!

With the dreadful week Ray experienced with Louise, he needed a vacation too. From the time I started planning my trip to Florida to visit my daughter, Jessica, I felt guilty for leaving him stuck at home. Louise would be a challenge, but never in my wildest dreams could I have predicted our area would have been hit by such a weather cataclysm. Sheets of rain were constant, never lessening to sprinkles. Nature's wrath dragging out that entire week compounded Louise's phobias. Things probably would have gone better for Ray if the weather cooperated.

June blended into July. The wet week subsided and a hot, muggy summer in central Pennsylvania surfaced. I cherished my days at home, free of schoolwork and juggling the demands of a teacher. Squeezing household duties into mornings before school, I became an expert at multi-tasking. During the school year, the washer spun as I scrubbed the kitchen floors on my hands and knees. Brownies baked in the oven at 7:30 a.m. while I showered. The dishwasher hummed as I corrected one last set of the previous night's homework papers. Before I rushed out the door, I answered numerous Furry Friends Network emails as I watched the computer's clock. My colleagues remarked they got tired just listening to all I accomplished before 8:00 a.m. during school days. I did not miss that hectic school year schedule one bit. Now, I savored a cup of java, daring to add a touch of coffee liqueur. Leisure sips replaced downright gulps during the school year while I viewed *Good Morning America* on television. Now, sitting on the couch, I stroked Louise's soft fur. I relished the time with my beagles. Morning walks once crammed into predawn hours prior to my school day were currently relaxing strolls. Summers off – a big advantage of being a teacher.

Ray did not feel as relieved. His summer days consisted of spending long hours laboring in the heat. He arrived home grimy and sweaty from restoring boilers in furnace rooms where temperatures topped one hundred degrees. Squeezing his two-hundred-pound plus body, Paul Bunyan physique, in places just big enough for a cat to fit through, he performed backbreaking repairs. Black soot on his face made him resemble a coal miner. Or, he bent over all day welding gas lines in dusty, dirt ditches.

Although he had a lucrative livelihood, Ray's stressful days and physical demands were getting the best of him. Rings of white salt stains saturated his blue denim work shirts from excessive perspiration. With only one kidney, I worried if he drank enough water on those torrid days. To make matters worse, he did not have the option of wearing seasonal attire. A welder's wardrobe consists of heavy clothing and long sleeves year round to protect him from sparks and burns. Plus, he wasn't getting any younger. Popping over the counter pain pills became a habit as his left hip ached from crawling in trenches. His arthritic hands were stiff and sore as he flexed his fingers in and out to loosen the joints. Pursuing the American Dream was going to be the demise of my workaholic husband. Not only was Ray's work manual, but he also dealt with the headaches of owning a business. Hiring dependable employees, maintaining equipment, administrative work, compiling payroll, and billing were some of the never-ending duties required to run a smooth operation. Ray needed a respite from his toil.

Ray and I both dedicated ourselves to our professions for over twenty-five years. We do little for entertainment throughout the year. We don't frequent expensive restaurants or go to the movies often. Our usual Saturday night enjoyment is watching reruns of *Cops* on television. Call us homebodies. We're a meat and potatoes kind of couple. We are content living a simple, perhaps frugal, existence. We don't exactly rock in our rocking chairs on the front porch and strum the tune to *Deliverance* on our banjos, but we spend warm evenings sitting outside on our white wicker furniture with the hounds at our feet, nonetheless.

As for me, I don't ask for much in life. I use coupons at the grocery store, hunt bargain games and prizes for my class at yard sales, and buy my clothes from the clearance or reduced rack. Designer clothes are overpriced. Tanning would be considered splurging. Spoiling myself at a spa doesn't interest me. Something inside me restrains me from self-indulging or treating myself to fine wine and a fancy lifestyle. Because I never ask for anything, Ray and our daughters have a hard time finding gifts to give me for Mother's Day, birthdays and Christmas. A ten-dollar frying pan and a rug cleaner (to clean the dog pee out of the rugs) are examples of my wish list. My family gives me heck because I am too practical and down to earth.

"You're too hard to buy for," Ray complained before my upcoming birthday in July. "How about a gift certificate to get your nails done?" he suggested.

"I can't tolerate the chemical smells in nail salons. My sinuses would kill me," I answered.

"There must be something you've always wanted," Ray said. "Stop worrying about spending too much money. The sky's the limit. And it can't be a gift for the house or the dogs. It has to be just for you."

After a few days of sleeping on it, I decided what to ask for as my birthday present. *I'll show him who's too practical*, I thought.

"I know what I want for my birthday," I said to Ray one evening while making tacos for supper.

"What? And don't ask for something trivial such as a casserole dish or a new collar for Louise," he ordered. "Be extravagant!"

"Alrighty then. Want to know what I want? I've always wanted to go to Hawaii. It's been my lifelong desire. Before I die, I want to see Hawaii. How's that for extravagant?" I said, wondering what his reaction would be. "And, you need a break from your work before you keel over."

After Ray got over the initial shock of my uncharacteristic request, he said, "That's not a bad idea. Hawaii, eh?"

We toyed with the idea of our lavish vacation for the next few days. I surfed the Internet, browsed ports of call, and priced package deals. Rental car vs. no car, which islands to visit, stateroom or garden villa, how long a trip, what cruise lines to consider. Not really intending for it to be a reality, I searched for the perfect vacation, figuring it was still a dream.

The following day, Ray walked in the door at 7:00 p.m. after repairing a backhoe. "It's sweltering out there," he said.

"The dogs and I stayed in the air conditioning most of the day," I said with reluctance. Taking off his grubby hat, he wiped the sweat off his forehead with his sleeve. He carefully placed his work boots, soiled with grease, on the throw rug by the door. He was beat. As he walked past me in the kitchen and reached for a cold beer, he said, "Let's do it."

"Do what?" I asked, thinking he meant performing some household chore such as cutting the grass.

"Go to Hawaii. It's time we live it up a little," said Ray. "Life is too short. I've got to do something else besides bust my butt every day."

"For real? You're not kidding? I didn't think you liked the sand and being out in the sun," I said.

"We're going. Get your grass skirt and coconut bra packed," Ray commanded with a chuckle.

With those instructions, I booked a ten-day cruise to Hawaii in July. It toured three islands beginning at Honolulu, Oahu. Our newly christened 2,466-passenger cruise ship was only three months old. It was acclaimed as the largest and most expensive U.S.-flagged passenger vessel built in its time. Complete with casino, saunas, hot tubs, tennis court, library, theatre, freestyle dining, ten restaurants, and other amenities, our ship awaited.

The only caveat was what to do about Louise.

We arranged for Ray's sister, Donna Crist, to stay at the house and dog sit our other two beagles, Riley and BuddyLee. That was no problem. But Louise couldn't remain home this time. Donna was not expected to deal with Louise's mental state, fear of humans, and frequent potty needs. Donna is good with dogs, but it was out of the question for us to stick Louise with any *reasonable* person.

Well, I am not saying my good friend, Stephanie Grossnickle, is an *unreasonable* person. But, I felt comforted knowing that my Furry Friends Network comrade once again offered to help us take a vacation. I could think of no one else who had such excellent experience with rescue dogs.

"Hawaii? You lucky girl," Stephanie commented when I asked her to watch Louise.

"Make sure you take Ray to a luau with hula dancers. He deserves it after the time he had when you were in Florida visiting Jessica."

"Yes, Ray kept his horrendous week a secret from me so I could enjoy myself with my daughter," I said. "He's overdue for some R & R."

About a week before we left, I arranged to have Louise visit Stephanie so that she could get accustomed to Stephanie and her home. "I think she remembers you," I said as Louise expressed an interest in sniffing Stephanie. She did not flee as though she was a horse being kicked by spurs. Louise's tail was glued to her behind, but her nose went to work. She explored new smells in Stephanie's fenced yard, performing a nasal exam, beagle style. Being mindful of anything where Louise could get into trouble, I noticed a gap under the gate where she could squeeze through if she wanted to get out. We placed landscape timbers to block the opening so our little escapee couldn't pull another Houdini stunt. Stephanie reassured me that she would keep a short leash on Louise inside the house to catch her this time. Having mostly hardwood flooring in her home, she wasn't troubled with accidents on the rugs.

A feeling of disquiet came over me because we'd be so far away if anything happened. "Maybe this is a bad idea," I said softly to Stephanie. "Maybe I should cancel our plans."

"I can always call Robin, head of Furry Friends Network, if there's a problem. The organization's vets have all her records. She'll be fine here, Sharon. She survived for almost three weeks on her own when she was loose. You and Ray need to treat yourselves. Don't you dare back out of this trip," Stephanie lectured me as I got back into my car. "I'll be happy to foster Louise."

Technically, Louise was still a Furry Friends Network foster dog. She wasn't really mine, although many acquaintances assumed I owned her. Louise wasn't advertised on the website, she was nowhere near ready to be adopted, but the rescue continued to pay her medical bills and provide me with dog food. I was still considered her guardian, providing a temporary home. There was still the hope that with continued work, Louise would become adoptable and find her forever home.

Back at my home on the Sunday before our departure date, my doubts and mixed feelings concerning the trip resurfaced. I started my preliminary travel chores by writing instructions for Donna, Ray's sister, our dog sitter. Then, in further preparation, I proceeded to clean out the refrigerator, and dragged our largest suitcase, with its wheels wobbling, up the steps to the bedroom. It was a typical lazy Sunday with ham and green beans stewing in the crockpot. Ray watched a stock car race on television and snoozed sporadically on the recliner. While I assembled a bag of travel toiletries, I could hear Ray's intermittent snores and gasps for air from upstairs. His week of hard work had caught up with him. After digging through my dressy summer clothes, saturated with that musty drawer smell from last year, I threw in a few loads of laundry to freshen them up. After sealing suntan lotion and shampoo in plastic bags, I packed our big, striped beach towels and a week's worth of cosmetics. Thinking ahead, I tied a bright pink ribbon on the suitcase to identify it more easily at the airport baggage claim.

Although it was a quiet day, Louise was more skittish than usual. She jerked at the snapping of bottle caps and the opening of suitcase latches. I swear she leaped ten feet from the chair as Ray's snorts startled her. Why was Louise unsettled and on edge? Her notorious pacing in circles signaled agitation and uncertainty. Every hour and a half, she urinated on the rugs even though I took her out frequently. Did Louise sense a change in routine? Could she possibly know we were going away?

While filling out the identification tag on our suitcase, a remark popped in my head, which haunted me. At a recent vet appointment, one of the vet technicians saw Louise's scared behavior. This worker commented to me, "Sharon, do you think Louise can really be happy? Is she ever normal?" Now, I looked at my disturbed little girl, shaking and jittery as she sniffed the luggage. *Can Louise ever be content in this world?* I thought. Then I remembered our deceased Nellie. I promised to never keep a dog alive just for me. Was it fair to keep Louise alive because I did not have the courage to put her down? Was her constant urinating her way of telling us life was too much for her to bear?

That day I said little to Ray about my hesitations but still agonized over whether or not to go on our dream vacation. We had deposited five thousand dollars for the trip of a lifetime. Even with travel insurance, could I say I'm canceling because my dog is nervous? I was willing to forfeit it all for Louise's best interest. Then I realized she may freak and be worse at Stephanie's, especially without me. More importantly, maybe there was a bigger decision to be made.

The next day I emailed Terri, our trainer, and Robin, our rescue leader, explaining Louise's behavior and the situation that plagued me. Robin agreed Louise may be devastated at Stephanie's. Terri told me that the ultimate act of love is letting go. I should do what's best for Louise. This crossroad moment was a life-altering decision. To help me resolve my quandary, Robin put me in touch with another pet communicator who gave advice to her when her own dog, Chase, suffered from severe medical problems. Chase, a boxer, endured everything from seizures to perforated stomach ulcers. Robin spent thousands of dollars on his care, hospitalizing him at the best veterinary universities. It was always touch and go with many close calls.

Before we left on our trip, I contacted the pet communicator, telling her limited information about Louise. She said she pictured a circle, half black and half white, which represented Louise's brain. Envisioning a motion picture reel running in fast speed, she sensed chaos and confusion. Running, racing, fleeing in perpetual woe. She perceived Louise's mental torment.

"I'm not getting a good feeling about this dog at all," she told me. "Her mind is jumbled and rattled. I see her in dark, closed, cramped quarters. Where did she come from?"

"She's a rescue dog," I answered. "I don't know much about her history."

With that, the pet communicator told me that Louise is indeed, a very distressed dog. The final resolution is mine. But if life is too much for Louise to handle, she needs to be at peace. We both knew what she meant.

When our conversation ended, I felt even more distraught. Did she picture Louise when she was at the shelter in West Virginia before she was my foster dog? Did she picture Louise when she was on the loose? Or, was Louise always running away from people and noise that scared her, away from life? Her statement about the closed quarters got me thinking. I always suspected Louise may have been used in lab experiments. Her inscrutable past made her a victim of her own circumstances. As I ran to my computer, my fingers couldn't type fast enough as I searched on the Internet for "beagles used in lab experiments." To my horror, beagles are the number one dog used in lab experiments because they are friendly, sweet, small, and easy to handle. I learned their docile dispositions make them perfect targets for vivisection, or the operating on live animals. An estimated 65,000 are used worldwide in everything from medical research, drug and food testing, and pharmacological trials. Barbaric methods conducted have been used to study maternal deprivation, painful surgical mutilation, effects of smoking, immune function, and pesticide toxicity. Forceful inhalation of poisonous chemicals was carried out as beagles jerked their heads away in protest and went into seizures. The color drained from my face as I read these injustices. Despite these actions, beagles are a breed that seldom complains. In my thirteen years of fostering, I've never come across a mean beagle, no matter what iniquities were done to them.

It made sense. The only time Louise would have been touched by humans is when they prodded or poked her, resulting in pain. The anticipation of the probe of a needle heightened her stress response and spiked her fight or flight reflex. That explained her intense fear of people. She was entirely unsocialized from being caged in dark, confined housing. Her neurotic symptoms justified her behavior. I could never prove it, but this suspicion ate away at me.

"Our new cruise ship may have to set sail without us," I told Ray hesitantly when he came home from work that day. "I don't know what to do about Louise."

Finding the courage to bring the subject to Ray's attention, I gave him the lowdown. Ray listened with distrust to the findings of the pet communicator about the possibility Louise may have been a laboratory beagle, to Terri's advice, and to the vet tech's comment. Voicing my apprehensions about leaving her, I suggested that Louise might not have the capability to be truly happy. Her frequent peeing was her way of conveying to us that she cannot be joyous in everyday life. Maybe I wasn't listening to her body signals. Maybe I turned my head the other way because I couldn't face the truth. Six months had passed since she came into our lives. She did not show the improvements or changes I expected. We had a physically healthy but otherwise, mentally anguished dog.

"I'm so torn," I told Ray quietly. "I don't know the answer."

"I know the answer," was Ray's immediate response. "How could you even consider such an idea? We didn't go through all that trying to find her for nothing. And besides, Louise is happy with us." He scowled at me as though I should be locked away in a loony bin. I hadn't seen that fuming look on Ray's face since Nellie dragged the gooey wax ring from the toilet all over the carpets.

Not one more word was spoken. Ray would not fathom the idea of putting Louise down. End of discussion. Case closed. I must have been berserk to suggest such a ridiculous notion. That solved that. Once again, Ray proved to be my voice of reason.

With closed lips about Louise, we finished packing for our trip over the next several days. Louise wasn't quite so jittery compared to how she acted that Sunday. Excited about leaving, Ray and I were busy with last minute details. Focusing on pre-trip errands, I engaged myself with purchasing a new swimsuit and formal wear, withdrawing our spending money, paying bills ahead of time, and printing flight schedules for family members.

The night before the trip, I dropped off Louise at Stephanie's. The vet recommended doubling Louise's anxiety medication for this short period of time. Still questioning her well-being in the back of my mind, I forced myself to follow through with my vacation plans.

"You go and have a good time," Stephanie insisted while she pushed me back into my car Louise-less. "And practice swiveling those hips for your hula lessons."

With a sinking heart, I bade farewell to Louise. As I drove home dispirited, I pondered going to Hawaii and almost turned back around to pick up Louise.

The big day arrived. The clock radio beeped as Ray reached over, grappled for its annoying button, and slammed it down. Awakening at 3:00 a.m., we stumbled over Riley and BuddyLee in the dark and stammered our way downstairs to brew a pot of coffee. I resisted the urge to phone Stephanie in the middle of the night and check on Louise. Was Louise asleep? Did Louise miss me? Was Louise getting along with the other dogs?

This was my last chance to back out.

Beagle Bit

Since its inception in 2010, the Beagle Freedom Project has found loving homes for about 150 beagles who spent their lives as test subjects in research facilities. Please go online and sign the Beagle Freedom Bill, which promotes "Life After Labs."

Chapter Sixteen

Aloha Hawaii!

At 6:00 a.m., Harrisburg International Airport buzzed with activity. Travelers rushed to their gates while sipping flavored coffees, announcements blaring in the terminal echoed in our ears, suitcase wheels glided friction free on the smooth tile floors, and patrons chatted on their cell phones. *Who can they be talking to at this hour?* I wondered.

Maybe it wasn't too early to phone Stephanie to check on Louise. The ticket line snaked in and out of routed rails. Standing the 34th person in line, I imagined I was back at the theme park queue lines in Florida.

The flight from Harrisburg to Chicago was effortless. But the nine-hour trip from Chicago to Honolulu tested our endurance. *Now I know how an astronaut feels,* I thought as my legs stiffened and my back ached. I wiggled my butt to relieve my fidgetiness. The airplane seat felt like it was stuffed with rocks. Ray stretched his limbs by taking frequent walks up and down the aisle. To help pass the time and prohibit me from obsessing about Louise, I absorbed myself in reading the book *Marley & Me* by John Grogan.

Passengers turned around and stared at me as I burst out laughing at Marley's antics. At least Louise never ate an eighteen karat gold necklace[3] or busted out of her cage. After I concealed my face in the pages and roared another chortled outbreak, I peeked over the cover and said to those around me, "Great book, you ought'a read it." Or I nudged Ray as I chuckled and said, "Read this part. Maybe Louise isn't so bad after all. Look what he put up with from his yellow Lab."

If I'd ever meet the author in person, I'd say, "Oh, John, I feel your pain. What we go through for our dogs!" Marley suffered from severe separation anxiety. He chewed through crates and walls during thunderstorms, having brontophobia, fear of thunder that causes anxiety, like Louise. His unruliness and disobedience deemed him "the world's worst dog" by his owner. Barreling through the house, he acted like a stampeding elephant in a dog's body. But being a dedicated pet parent, John's love for Marley prevailed. We can all learn from this man's commitment to his dog. He never

---

3 John Grogan, page 100.

gave up on Marley. Maybe I did the right thing, I thought. I'll never give up on Louise, either, I vowed. But I suppose my little Louise could be credited with "the world's most scared dog." I read the entire book in one cramped, stationary sitting. As I finished reading the book and shut the novel, the captain announced, "Welcome to the Aloha State!"

Tour guides greeted us at the airport as they draped purple and white leis over our necks. The fragrance of fresh irises aggravated my allergies, but I didn't dare take off my Hawaiian accessory. Everyone was decked out in their resplendent flowered shirts, straw hats, and moo moos. How I wished for a head of that dark, thick beautiful hair and the year round bronzed skin that the Polynesian people possess.

We were not hampered by our long day of flying and six hour time difference. No jet lag for the Crees! We were ready to rock n' roll. Waikiki Beach was even more beautiful than the brochures' pictures. Clean sand, glistening turquoise ocean water, and volcanic mountains in the distance draped the land. Similar to Las Vegas, Honolulu came alive at night. Street vendors, musicians, jugglers, dancers, jokesters, and singers had a designated spot on every block. Some dressed up like the Statue of Liberty or spray-painted themselves silver like the Tin Man in the *Wizard of Oz* movie. Packs of people roamed the sidewalks and gathered around the entertainment. These one-man shows dazzled us by their talent and unusual amusement. We sauntered the town until the wee hours of the morning.

We arose early for our day at Pearl Harbor, located at the other end of the island of Oahu. Reading a history book cannot replace the awe and dolefulness we experienced in person. Knowing that we stood above entombed servicemen, patriotism welled up in our hearts. Tourists shuffled in silence in the memorial over the sunken USS Arizona battleship as it continued to ooze oil since it sunk. Petroleum still bubbled to the surface and formed a rainbow slick. This was the final resting place for 1,177 crewmen who lost their lives on December 7, 1941, as a Japanese kamikaze pilot flew into the hull of the ship. In this somber place, visitors shed tears as they read military personnel's names inscribed on a white marble wall. Occasional sniffles echoed in the shrine room as people mourned for their fallen brothers unbeknownst to them. Teaching Veteran's Day to my students would now have new meaning.

The battleship USS Missouri sat on Ford Island in the heart of Pearl Harbor. Drawn to the mechanics and fabrication of metal construction, Ray inspected its welds as we toured this warship. The USS Missouri would be 332 feet taller than the Washington Monument if it stood end to end. Moored along Battleship Row, the "Mighty Mo" staged the signing of Japan's surrender on September 2, 1945, which ended World War II. As amateur history buffs, we learned that gun turrets were turned toward Tokyo in case of trickery. I could only imagine the tension General Douglas MacArthur felt during this world-changing event. Gunmen were ready to pull the trigger on their sixty-seven foot long gun barrels and unleash "Mighty Mo's" power if need be. I realized the enormity of war as we saw a colossal anchor that weighed thirty-one thousand pounds. Each of its chain links weighed one hundred ten pounds. "That chain link weighs as much as you do," Ray teased me.

"Not if I keep eating my way through this vacation," I replied. Standing on the Surrender Deck, I felt proud to be an American.

The next day we boarded our 965-foot-long cruise ship. You couldn't miss it. It was about the biggest thing I'd ever seen. Decorated with colorful hibiscus, Hawaii's state flower painted on its exterior, it looked like a floating rainbow. Mirrors glistered, polished brass handrails sparkled, and spotless glass doors (minus smudges and dog froth that my own glass doors included) lined the lounges. I sipped my Blue Hawaiian drink at the bar while listening to the music of the baby grand piano. *This sure beats life in Dauphin*, I thought. We slept like hibernating bears as the darkness of the cabin and the subtle rocking of the ship perpetuated a sound sleep. No choking on dog fur, paws poking in our backs, or arising at 6:00 a.m. to let dogs out. Most mornings I jogged around the promenade of the ship for my exercise like a normal person without the aggravation of three beagles tugging me forward.

But even though it was gratifying to be away, down deep I missed my beagles, aggravation and all, especially Louise. We sent Stephanie an email from the ship, under the presumption it was a friendly hello and update of our trip. But Stephanie, of course, sensed my uneasiness over Louise. Harried by thoughts that Louise was not adjusting or had escaped under the fence, I had to put my mind at rest. Stephanie replied the next day with favorable news. Louise was doing as good as could be expected. Although restless and somewhat out of sorts, she was eating, sleeping through the night, and accepting treats. She avoided Stephanie's attempts at gentle touches, but followed the pack of foster dogs out into the yard to run and play. What a comfort to know that Louise was safe and sound. And now I could breathe a sigh of relief, or at least try to.

You can't take a cruise without mentioning the food. Ray and I tried a different cuisine every night. I ordered foods from the menu I couldn't even pronounce. Remembering from taking three years of French in high school, I did not request the escargots. From crepes to creoles to sushi to eggroll to steak, we waddled our way out of each restaurant, including the Aloha Cafe smorgasbord. *Fitting into my bathing suit might be a challenge*, I thought. So to compensate, sometimes I ate fruit. The Hawaiian pineapple was unlike any I ever tasted. I couldn't get enough of it. Sweet, juicy, ripe and fresh, I craved it morning, noon, and night. It's nothing like the canned pineapple you buy in the grocery store on the mainland. Deep golden in color, it melted in my mouth. So while I gorged on pineapple, Ray consumed at least a pound a day of chocolate-covered macadamias. Native to Hawaii, macadamias are Ray's favorite nut (besides me!). Being coffee lovers, we guzzled several cups a day of farm grown Kona coffee cultivated in Hawaii. Its rich, robust flavor made me want another mug. No wonder I had so much energy for the nightlife.

One evening on the ship while sipping our java, the captain summoned us on deck to observe a sight. We were on route from Hilo, Hawaii to Kahului, Maui. Burning orange lava flowed into the sea from Mount Kilauea. Active volcanoes are something you read about in a *National Geographic* magazine or see in a documentary on television. The oozing red rivers of molten rock sizzled as the ocean swallowed them. Mother Nature's changes and geological forces were a miracle to witness.

Hawaii was a paradise on earth. I couldn't believe with all the fruit and flowers, there were no bugs or insects. At home in Pennsylvania, my back porch was infiltrated with stink bugs. They littered the screens by the hundreds. And being allergic to bee stings, I was on the lookout for yellow jackets and wasps. One summer, I ran over a nest of yellow jackets in the ground with the riding mower and they swarmed after me. Now, armed with several allergy medicines, I was prepared for the buzzing creatures. But there were none.

Speaking of buzzing, Ray and I had a blast conversing with the locals. Hawaiians are the friendliest, most sincere, courteous people I've ever met. Our bus drivers not only related tourist facts and information about the islands, but related to us on a personal level. One man told of being forced to attend an English speaking school when Hawaii became a state. Another driver relayed to us that it took three feet of sugar cane to make one packet of table sugar. I'll always think of those burnt sugar cane fields when I put a teaspoon of sugar in my coffee.

In spite of all our fun, down deep I fretted over Louise. I didn't let Ray know she was always in the back of my mind. Days the ship was out to sea, there was no Internet access. But days the ship pulled into port, I snuck to the computers and emailed Stephanie to check on Louise. While Ray was at the ship's casino, I made the excuse I wasn't much of a gambler. Then I snuck back to the computers to see if Stephanie replied. It was a relief to me when Stephanie reported that Louise got along with all the other dogs and enjoyed nosing in her backyard.

Of all the excursions we booked from the ship, we thought we'd relive our childhood so we signed up for a downhill bike ride. Our tour van traveled up miles and miles of winding, red canyon roads. It took almost two hours to reach our destination. I must have been out of my mind for signing up for this outing. It had been at least thirty-five years since I had ridden a bicycle. After zigzagging from side to side but passing a preliminary riding test, I strapped on my helmet and began my descent. Wobbling and unsure of myself, I slowed down the entire brigade as an experienced biker to my rear cursed me. We zoomed down curves like a roller coaster. With breakneck speed, pedaling wasn't necessary as gravity pulled us down, down, down the steep slopes. We picked up momentum like a freight train. I don't know how fast we flew or how far we declined. I just wanted off the darn thing! Losing control around a turn, I veered into the middle of the street instead of staying on the white line. I applied the hand brakes all too often as I prayed the nightmare would soon be over. How I didn't manage to fall and break my head open, crash and land in a ditch, or fly off a cliff remains a mystery. Ray said I resembled the Wicked Witch of the West in the *Wizard of Oz* movie, hunched over and pedaling her two-wheeler. I was so sick at the end of this ordeal, it's a wonder *my* face wasn't green.

The next day I shopped for souvenirs, with my feet planted firmly on a foundation, while Ray took an ATV trip. "I'll appreciate being grounded and enjoy myself spending money today. You go by yourself," I told him. "I've had enough cycling, motorized or not, to last a lifetime."

This time with four wheels, Ray drove an all-terrain vehicle at Haleakala Ranch on the island of Maui. Amazed to learn that cattle ranches are a main industry in Hawaii, Ray geared up for his adventure. The tour guide, native to the mainland, gave a safety orientation to first time riders. But Ray had all that experience downhilling from the day before. It's a good thing he had a jacket along as the weather turned chilly and it began to sleet. Imagine that, snow in Hawaii! That didn't interfere with his wild undertaking as he jumped hills, did donuts, and spun in the mud yelling, *"Yee Haw!"*

"Hey, Cowboy, pack your swim trunks," I said to Ray the following day. "We're going swimming with sea turtles at Molokini Crater." Since I loved to snorkel, seeing the brilliant tropical fish and unusual coral was a highlight of our vacation for me. Maneuvering like a mermaid with my flippers propelling me, I gazed at the splendors of ocean life. When Ray jumped off the boat, he ingested a mouthful of seawater. Then his goggles loosened, flooding his vision with murkiness. I was lucky enough to spot several sea turtles, while Ray didn't see any. "What were they doing?" he asked as he came up from the water and removed his facemask.

"Playing cards, silly, what do you think they were doing?" I quipped as a payback for his Wicked Witch comment about my bicycling skills. *I ain't no champion cyclist, but you're no Jacques Cousteau,* I thought.

We traded in our snorkeling gear for our formal wear since the dress up dinner was that night. Clad in my mint green, silky evening gown, diamond stud earrings (really cubic zirconia), stiletto heels, and matching sequin clutch bag, I felt like a princess. My handsome hubby looked swank in his suit and tie compared to his usual denim and thick workman's welding attire. I joked that the last time I saw him dressed up in his Sunday best was for a funeral.

"I clean up pretty good," my debonair Ray said as he pulled my chair out for me at the dinner table. It was our final night on the cruise. After we figured out what all the forks were for, we ate a delectable seven-course meal.

"Better eat your fill now," I warned. "Don't expect this kind of service at home," I joked.

"Yep, it's back to reality," Ray said as he spooned me one last bite of chocolate mousse.

"I want to come back to Hawaii. There's so much we didn't do like the waterfall hike, the Circle of Fire helicopter excursion, and the glass bottom boat ride," I said as we returned to our room.

Ray answered by hanging the Do Not Disturb sign on our cabin door. "Better enjoy one more night of no dogs in bed," he said. Tired from all that swimming and that big meal, we promptly fell asleep.

From botanical gardens to black lava rock beaches, all good things must come to an end. It was time to check out our bags and head home after ten days of Hawaiian bliss. We had corresponded with Stephanie a few more times throughout the trip. She told us that Louise was doing all right. This gave me a continued spark of hope for Louise. We made the right decision to sustain her life and keep her in ours.

Our flight back to the mainland was overnight, but I didn't sleep much. Uncomfortable in the airplane seat, I nodded off and took brief catnaps. Slumping over and leaning on Ray's shoulder in the airport, I tried to catch a few snoozes during the layover in Chicago. When we arrived back in Pennsylvania, I did not have my land legs yet. Ray chuckled at my swaying movements. Because I got limited sleep, I felt woozy and dizzy. But I did not want to go home to nap. The way I felt didn't keep us from making one important stop on the way home.

We went straight to Stephanie's home to pick up Louise. Stephanie was surprised to see Louise come to life and wag her tail for the first time. "Oh, Sharon, look how much she missed you," commented Stephanie as Louise slobbered me with kisses. We chatted about the trip and how Louise fared during her stay. Louise was a nose on four legs as she ran through Stephanie's yard probing the ground like an anteater on steroids. Stephanie tempted Louise with pieces of turkey to win her confidence. Louise snatched the bait and even stayed close to Stephanie at times. After some fearful cowering, Louise eventually sat beside Stephanie on the couch. Stephanie remained still to gain her reliance. By the end of ten days, Louise allowed Stephanie to pet her without making any sudden moves. Stephanie realized this was a breakthrough. Louise had the capacity to trust another human being. Stephanie loved our little girl as much as we did.

"You sure have one special little dog," Stephanie proclaimed as we loaded Louise into the car and thanked her profusely.

As I made my unsteady walk to our vehicle, I answered, "She's one of a kind, that's for sure. We wouldn't want it any other way!"

Beagle Bit

The U.S. Dept. of Agriculture uses over sixty beagle teams in twenty-one international airports across the U.S. The Beagle Brigade is responsible for sniffing out and confiscating fruits, vegetables, hidden plants, and meats that are banned from crossing the country's borders. Most dogs work for the Brigade for 6 – 10 years.

Chapter Seventeen

Louise Becomes a "Cree-gle"

After our Hawaiian vacation, relaxing as it was, it was obvious what our feelings and love for Louise were. We realized how Louise, with all of her fears and phobias, had grown into our hearts. Who were we kidding? We didn't want it any other way, and we didn't want Louise going anywhere else. We wanted her to be our very own scared and neurotic beagle, a "Cree-gle," as we called our own beagles.

Louise's bio write up and picture were not advertised on our Furry Friends Network website of dogs and cats that were available for adoption. Even so, Robin had been holding out for months, hoping that Louise could be advertised for adoption and placed in her forever home. Terri's goal, as the Furry Friends Network trainer, was that Louise could be rehabilitated and be given to that special person who could understand her fears. But with how I worried and fussed over Louise going to Stephanie's for ten days while we were in Hawaii, I could never surrender her to an adopter. Even though I became acquainted with my potential applicants quite well, I could never consider the idea of Louise transitioning into a new environment. Nor would I want to give the public the idea that a rescue dog is a bad choice as a pet because it has severe issues. Louise's case is what we term a "forever foster" – a dog too old, too sick, or with extreme behavioral problems. The "forever foster" rescue dog just simply cannot be adopted. Those cases are few and far between compared to the many wonderful rescue dogs that find good forever homes. The beagles that I have rescued and helped, over fifty in all, and continue to welcome into my foster care to this day, have all been adopted successfully. But we had come to know and accept, that Louise needed to reside with us, at our home. That was fine with Ray and me.

Every other foster dog I've had has been able to adjust to his permanent setting with an adoptive family in a matter of days, just like the adjustment it has to make when I first bring it to my house. Sure, it may be a little unsettled and must learn a different routine, but the dog quickly adapts to his surroundings. Favorable updates and emails from adopters of rescue dogs, claiming the dog acclimated and rapidly became a new member of the family, are the norm. Rescue dogs are amazing in the way they rebound and establish trust with humans so rapidly.

After I carry out an adoption and all the necessary papers are signed, I hand over the leash to the other party who will be the foster dog's new forever home. The new approved owners receive their goody bag of dog treats and toys that Furry Friends Network provides for them. Then I watch my foster dog wagging its tail, walking down the aisles of the adoption event at a pet retail store like he is strutting in a dog show with his familiar handler. He traipses off happy-go-lucky and jumps in the car with his new owner. No questions asked. It's like they're bosom buddies already. I am tempted to shout, "Hey, remember me? I'm the one who saved you. Aren't you going to turn around and at least say good-bye after I'm standing here bawling my eyes out?" It's what fostering is all about, preparing the rescue dog for his or her forever home. And, it makes me very happy each time a beagle I foster finds that perfect home.

But after seven months of fostering Louise, she would still never prance off in the arms of a newcomer to her subsequent life without a care in the world. I would not expect the ordinary family to succumb to such a needy dog with all of her fears and phobias. It was senseless to imagine Louise conforming to a strange dwelling. In our home, Louise had learned to prosper to the best of her ability.

Even after all the grief she put us through, we decided Louise should unequivocally belong to us. After everything we did to get her back when she was on the loose, we felt we'd never let her go. All the blood, sweat, and tears we poured into her were to our avail. Ray and I became her safety net and impelled her chance of thriving in this world. We were all that she had. We broke the mold when she overcame her barrier of fear with us. Louise learned to love and rely on her foster parents, the two humans on earth in which she put her faith…Ray and me.

Louise was unhappy leaving the security and confines of our home, even after seven months of fostering. Taking her for a car ride or attempting to walk her in a different neighborhood still led to a calamity. Louise wanted to get out of there as fast as she could, as if she wished that she had an ejector button. She was out of her comfort zone. In good conscience, I could never have placed Louise elsewhere.

You may be thinking, *what's the big deal? Why wasn't she ours already?*

You see, Robin had placed me on fostering probation. No, not because I was a lousy foster mom, but because I was a good one. She didn't want to lose me.

"Too many hounds need your help, Sharon," Robin told me after Ray and I adopted our last rescue foster beagle, BuddyLee. "No more Furry Friends Network dogs can live permanently at the Cree household."

We adopted BuddyLee when Nellie was still alive. We hoped he'd be a playmate for our other beagle, Riley, since they were close in age. But BuddyLee did not turn out to be much of a social butterfly.

"I agree," I said at the time. "We're up to three beagles now, Nellie, Riley, and BuddyLee. I really do not want any more than that. I can handle three beagles of my own and still continue to foster."

That's what happens when you foster rescue dogs. You love them all, become attached, and want to keep each and every one of them. We in rescue call that dog a "keeper." Yes, it is hard to give them up even after a thorough application process, knowing they are going to a good home. But you can't adopt them all. As a foster, you can end up with multiple dogs of your own, the numbers get too big, and you stop fostering. Robin wanted to prevent that from happening with all of her good foster parents. She was a smart cookie. Too many canines in the house become hard to manage and lead to problems in the pack dynamics. Many townships also have local ordinances on the number of dogs permitted in a residence. Or, you have so many dogs to take care of, the foster dog that needs housetrained and obedience training doesn't get individual attention.

Louise received my undivided attention all right. She just about turned my life upside down! So here I was, asking for more challenges with Louise. A lifetime more of Louise. Ray and I invested so much effort in her future that her future belonged with us.

We officially adopted Louise on September 26, 2006, nine months after she arrived in that transport and we welcomed her into our home as a foster dog. Maybe she was sent to replace our old Nellie girl, we'll never know. Louise did not accompany us to the adoption event at the pet supply store to complete the adoption paperwork. A public place with noises, barking dogs, and a large number of people would have been too traumatizing for her. So we signed our John Hancock's on the dotted line as Robin handed us our adoption goody kit loaded with dog toys and treats.

"You're the proud parents once again of a rescue dog," Robin said as she shook our hands and congratulated us on our new addition. "Louise is yours forever now."

"Louise always was ours," I said. "Now she's a bona fide 'Cree-gle.' That's a new breed

I invented for the beagles that get to set up occupancy with the Crees!"

Robin just laughed. "You and your beagles, Sharon. That magic touch you have with these dogs makes you the best beagler I know. You have truly earned your title of 'Beagle Lady'!"

As we exited the adoption event at the pet chain store with our armful of doggy doo-dads, I glanced at all the other Furry Friends Network dogs who were available for adoption and needed forever homes. They barked, wagged their tails, and licked the faces of prospective family members. Greeting people, jumping, and pulling to sniff the store's customers, their body language said, "Pick me! Pick me!"

"I wish we could have brought Louise here," I said to Ray as we were leaving the pet warehouse store with our official adoption papers. "I wish she could act like them," I said, pointing to the dogs inside as we walked to our vehicle.

"She wouldn't be Louise then. And we wouldn't have adopted her," Ray stated with his get 'er done attitude as he turned on the car's ignition.

I probably knew in my heart on that cold day in December when Louise stepped off the transport that she would be ours forever. That terrified little beagle was so distinctive from all my other fosters. There was something exceptional about Louise as soon as I spotted her. Our lives became attached the moment those frightful eyes met mine.

Louise was here to stay. Louise was in her forever home.

Louise was with Ray and me, where she belonged.

Beagle Bit

Famous people who've owned beagles: Eva Gabor, Sara Gilbert, George Hamilton, James Herriot, President Lyndon B. Johnson, Barry Manilow, Mary Pickford, Charles Schultz and Roger Staubach.

Chapter Eighteen

Life with Louise Today

You can't teach an old dog new tricks, so they say. "Sure you can," I say. You can't teach a demented and neurotic beagle coping skills and tactics to deal with the world, they might say. Well, maybe that is partly true, I will admit. Louise's hard won accomplishments, even though they may have been considered slight strides in normal dogs, were something for which Ray and I remained grateful. It took six months before Louise would let Ray leash her, as just one example. Learning the doggy steps to our bed, walking by the sliding glass door, and eagerly hopping into the car were virtual triumphs, taking many months to achieve. But Louise's intense fear of people encompassed our lives for the longest time, and now, many years later, although better, still exists. At best, Louise snatched treats grudgingly from strangers, but being a sociable dog was not in her DNA from whatever her early life experiences were. Fear festered like a cancer in Louise. How was I going to find a cure for it? And, more likely, would I *ever* find a cure for it?

Louise's achievements were not as dramatic as my other foster dogs', which arrived and exited our house as though moving through a revolving door. Every few weeks a new beagle entered the Cree household, each with its own personality and story to tell. They all had their quirks. While riding in the car, one foster beagle ducked his head every time we drove under a bridge! Another had the idiosyncrasy of purring like a cat at mealtime. Some were abused and starved; others were strays in heat. A few were victims of castoffs of owners who did not have time for them. And occasionally, a hound dog would arrive at our doorstep to foster, despondent and rejected, taken to a shelter or abandoned by its owner simply because it had refused to hunt. But all overcame their physical hardships and emotional baggage in an astonishing and rapid manner. Loving people, families wanting to help a rescue dog, accepted each of these beagles into their forever homes without a hitch. Each time, I took one last look into those coffee brown eyes of my foster dog, filled with graceful solace, as it embarked on its next journey in life. One by one, I watched my fosters trot off into the sunset with their adoptive families as though they were old chums. Mission accomplished. My job was done.

But my job was not finished with Louise. I finally admitted to myself, my job with Louise might never be finished. Her topaz eyes continued to exhibit frenzy and fret at everyday occurrences, primarily humans and noises. Even though she was a permanent member of our household and I did not have to be concerned with adopting her out, I wanted Louise to be happy. I did not want to sustain a wretched dog's life. It would be unfair to have her live incongruous to our world. How could I better wheedle the woes of this whacked out dog? I was determined to keep trying.

The answer was the walks. According to Cesar Millan, the walk is the best job you can give your dog.[4] Walks were the key force in eking out Louise's assurance. Pulling on the leash as a normal dog would, she experienced unbridled enthusiasm unseen in other settings. When Louise was on walks, she could be an ordinary beagle; she would even rub her nose on the ground until it was almost raw following interesting scents. For a dog, smelling is the equivalent of feeling. A hike around our cul-de-sac could be compared to a trip around the world for the dogs. Every time! In the first six months that we had her, Louise showed the most improvement on our walks. The word "walk" had to be spelled, not said aloud. If she was in earshot, I'd better change into my walking shoes!

Weeks of walking drained into many months. Months spiraled into several years. Does time heal all wounds? Perhaps not all, but I rejoiced in whatever tiny feats Louise showed. If she gained a centimeter closer to another human or did not react to the sizzling of a hamburger frying, I reacted as though I'd won the lottery. But most days were uneventful and life rolled on. Typical days of teaching, performing household duties, caring for a large property, hosting holiday dinners, fostering, taking care of my own dogs, summers passing all too fast, and raising funds for Furry Friends

---

4 Cesar Millan, *Cesar's Way, The Natural, Everyday Guide to Understanding & Correcting Common Dog Problems*, page 213.

Network dictated my life. In spite of my busy schedule, I always made time for my daily saunters with Louise, my other beagles and my foster beagles. Thundering paws ran to the front door as the clink, clink of the leashes signaled our outing. Louise's tail bingbonged against the door and swiped the faces of Riley and BuddyLee as she anticipated our excursions in the neighborhood. The bevy of beagles exited our front door with explosive force. It didn't matter how many times a day we left. The dogs acted like a kid going to the circus at every single departure.

"You'll wear out the road!" my mailman yelled from his truck one day.

"We're on Louise Lane!" I hollered back. "We're just like you. Through rain, sleet, snow or hail..." So up and down the road we padded, several times a day, never missing an opportunity to rehabilitate Louise. We traveled the same beaten path, hoping to abate Louise's foibles. While Riley and BuddyLee stopped to water the mailbox posts, Louise surged onward with gallant strides. The walks ushered in a sense of canine confidence. Over the next several years, Louise changed from a scrambling scruff of fur to a streamlined streak of strength. Like a flower budding via time-lapse photography, but in slow motion, Louise's gradual growth blossomed before my eyes. My commitment and persistence paid off.

Nowadays, neighbors comment, "She's getting much better, isn't she, Sharon? She's not as afraid anymore."

"Yes, look at her now!" I gloat as Louise stands within a few inches of local diehard walkers whom we meet on our regular routine. Esther Edwards and I often pass each other on our early morning walks. Louise runs to her with doggy exuberance expecting a treat.

Or when our next-door neighbor, Bob Mastandrea, interrupted painting his shutters to declare, "Which one is Louise? I can't tell anymore."

Brad Coy, a neighbor who lives at the end of our block, commented just recently, "What a difference! You've done wonders with her!"

To our surprise, Louise has become somewhat of a neighborhood celebrity. Children run out their front doors, screen doors slamming, to greet Louise. "Can we try to pet her, Mrs. Cree?" they ask, fawning over her.

"Crouch down low and see if she'll approach you," I suggest to them. "Stay quiet and calm." Louise sniffs their hands for a moment, allowing a brief and gentle stroke. The kids smile with exultation that they had the honor of petting Louise.

In fact, Louise now just thinks she is "Little Miss All That." On the walks, and only on the walks, she has an attitude with a capital "A." Ray calls her "Walking Small" after the movie, *Walking Tall*. Our eighteen-pound bundle of nerves evolved into a muscular, midget of might who struts her stuff. The now extrovert Louise, on our walks, is a powerhouse that missiles through the fields, experiencing a world of excitement.

Noises that used to cause havoc are also diminishing for Louise. No more freaking out from the click, click of the nail clippers. I never could have imagined that Louise would now tolerate the buzzing sound while Ray prunes the bushes with an electric hedge trimmer. The whirring vibrations amazingly don't seem to bother her. She doesn't even flinch while I zoom by on the riding mower, hitting a tree root with a crack louder than a branch snapping. With raised hair on her back, she now barks at the garbage truck with a vengeance, lunging toward it while on her leash instead of running in the other direction as she did years ago. And who would have thought that inside the house, she stays in her stoic position on the couch while I run the vacuum cleaner? She thinks, *what, me get off this comfy sofa?* as I try to vacuum the dog hair off of it. She doesn't budge as I attempt to clean the cushions, this monster machine threatening to suck her up in the nozzle.

Ray and I have some longstanding jokes about Louise. One of them he doesn't even know about. One time I said, "Want a cookie?" while I was in the kitchen.

Ray hollered from our downstairs family room, "Sure, bring me some!" after I had served him a cup of coffee. I didn't have the heart to tell him I was talking to the dogs! So I graciously served him an assortment of cookies on a silver platter while winking at Louise.

Then the tables turned. When Ray arrived home from work one day he asked, "How's my Girlie, Girlie Goo?" making his voice two octaves higher.

Flattered I still appealed to him after twenty-four years of marriage as "his girl," I said, "I'm terrific!"

"That's good, but I was talking to Louise," he admitted.

Driving back home from a flea market one Sunday, Ray called our house on his cell phone. "Who are you calling?" I asked him, puzzled. "There's no one home. Remember, we're the only two people who live there. The girls moved out."

"I'm calling my little girl to tell her that we're on our way," Ray said with a smile.

So when we arrived home, I held the phone to Louise's ear so she could listen to the message. Louise cocked her head when she heard Ray's voice and could not understand how Ray got inside the phone. The silly things we do with our dogs. If you are a dog or cat or animal lover, I know you understand completely, and probably have done some crazy things like this yourself!

This next one falls into the category of either silly or ridiculous, not sure which one, or maybe a little of both. Not much has changed as far as our Saturday night entertainment and the Crees being homebodies. We still sit at home in the family room and watch reruns on television. Ray channel surfs and comments, "TV stinks tonight." But, the big difference is that Louise is fast asleep on the couch along with our other two beagles and whatever foster beagle or beagles might be living with us at the time. Louise walks behind the furniture throw on the couch, does an about-face, and cradles herself in the cover, with only her copper nose sticking out of the other end. Her calloused paws hang over the edge. All two to four dogs take up the entire sofa, comfortable and relaxed, while Ray and I sit on the hardwood floor, uncomfortable and squirmy. There's something wrong with this picture! They have us well trained, don't they? You, too? I can just see you shaking your head, understanding this situation perfectly!

There are times when, like our old dog, Nellie, Louise can even be naughty. Ray and I laugh at her antics, almost pleased that she can get in trouble like a normal dog. But Ray wasn't chuckling too much about this caper. One afternoon I arrived home from a demanding day at school. It began with a run in my stockings, an assembly had been cancelled, and rainy weather made for a noisy, indoor recess for energetic third graders. At the precise time of school's 4:05 p.m. dismissal, I had that, "I'm outta' here," frame of mind. Arriving home, I walked into my living room and discovered zillions of cassette tape ribbons, piled like mounds of spaghetti noodles. Oodles of shredded magnetic strips lined the stairway. Jagged pieces of plastic lay like shrapnel amongst the damage. Strings of evidence resembling dental floss stuck between Louise's teeth. Louise had decided to get into Ray's favorite country music selection, drag the tapes all out, and give them a try. Perhaps she prefers easy listening music to the country songs of Travis Tritt!

Then there's the time I was on the phone with Ray and heard *r-r-r-r-i-p!* The dogs were going through a crazy spell, flying in and out the pet door, running and chasing each other, sailing over steps like caped Super Dogs to burn off some excess energy. Louise and BuddyLee threw their foam pet beds, tossing and flipping them about like trained seals. "Wait a minute," I said to Ray while checking to make sure I hadn't split my pants, "that doesn't sound like foam tearing. I'd better go check what they're up to." Seems that Louise had grabbed the skirt at the bottom of the couch and ran with it. About four feet of flowered material dangled until I could remove the contraband from her mouth.

"You'll have another honey-do project tonight when you get home," I said with hesitation to Ray as I gawked at the flailing banner.

"Nothing a good staple gun can't fix," my devoted husband replied. Thank heavens he has a penchant and patience for beagles.

Because of his liking of the breed, Ray always invites a foster dog to jump up on the recliner with him during the evenings. Many fosters accomplish this the first few days they are in our care. Most dogs love to snuggle on a comfy chair, right? It took Louise a year and a half to feel valiant enough to nestle with Ray on his favorite man chair. Now I gaze over at her, nuzzled between him and the armrest, neck craned, snoring like a hibernating bear. Ray and I kid she snores so loud that we're going to buy her nasal strips. Ensconced with her Daddy, she is in doggy dreamland.

On the flip side, Louise developed a habit that has become a nightmare. I tried for eight long months to teach Louise to use the pet door. I do not encourage the fosters learning this device since most homes do not have one, but many dogs follow Riley or BuddyLee's lead within the first week. They enjoy the freedom to gain access inside and outside to the small section of our yard, which is fenced-in. Although she is housetrained, Louise still piddles frequently. It would be nice to have her go in and out on her own, I reckoned. "You'll never get her to use that contraption," Ray said to me.

"Patience is a virtue, my dear husband," I replied. Day after day, I held up the heavy vinyl division so its flapping would not scare her. To begin with, I moved the curtain back and forth so she'd get used to the flinging. Then for weeks I would fling and flung. Tempting her, I wiled her with treats to step over the threshold. Month after month, I coaxed her through the doggy door like a mommy trying to get a toddler to eat his vegetables. And ta-da! One day Louise culled up the courage, pushed her quivering body through that plastic flap, and placed her paws on to new independence. The clouds parted, angels sang, bells chimed, and a beam of sunlight shone down on Louise from the heavens above! But alas, this has come back to haunt me. After all my efforts, it seems this triumph has backfired. Now, in a nanosecond, Louise flies out the pet door when I am not looking, only to go out and eat her droppings!

Yes, this vile behavior actually has a name – coprophagia. But I don't feel so bad. If it has been deemed a special condition worthy of a title, then plenty of other dogs must do it, too. It is believed dogs ingest their feces for several reasons. They may be lacking in a vitamin, they are attracted to the acrid smell, they may be underfed, they may have a medical problem, a dog may have gotten into trouble for defecating and wants to clean it up, and mama dogs consume their puppies' waste to keep the nest sanitary. Louise did not partake in this crass compulsion until after her escape. I theorize she ate her excrement to survive, getting whatever nourishment it offered. Dogs possess a natural scavenger behavior. I've tried all the remedies for this disgusting stinky snack – a high fiber diet, deterrents such as hot sauce on her scat, purchasing commercially designed pills for coprophagia, adding mints or meat tenderizer to her food, and antidepressants for her compulsive disorder. Nope. Nada. Nothing worked with Louise. The only sure fire cure the vet suggested was to clean up her droppings immediately. So here I am, in my flannel granny gown and pink fuzzy slippers, holding a flashlight at night searching for the prize piles while shivering in temperatures sometimes of what feels like twenty below zero. If I can't find them all, her addle breath says it all. Louise comes in the pet door smacking her chops after pigging out on poop. Maybe Louise thinks she invented a new flavor for a "poop-sicle"!

That's not all Louise devours. One time she gorged on a forty-four pound bag of dry dog food when we weren't looking. Miss Sneaky Pete bulldozed her way into the garage. It took months to desensitize her to the loud striking of the screen door, which she was once afraid of. Letting it hit softly a thousand times, I showed her the garage was a "good place" since it housed her food. Ah, yes, this daring dauntless dog now blasts open that dreaded door on her own. Nudging it with her nose, Louise pays no attention to its loud banging as it shuts. She's not letting a screen door separate her from a potential feast! So while Ray and I were busy outside shoveling snow, Louise helped herself. When we came in to warm up, we couldn't find Louise. There she lay on the cement floor of the garage, unable to move, her belly distended the size of a cantaloupe. Serves her right for getting her paws in the cookie jar!

Getting cookies is one of Louise's favorite past times. To build her self-confidence, I taught Louise simple commands, and she does a nice "sit up" for a treat. Louise could not attend obedience school at a public place, but it is important to teach dogs the basics. Dogs look to you for guidance and it builds the bond between the canine and you as pack leader. Getting rewarded for rudimentary tasks such as "sit, stay, and come" promotes a dog's assurance and that compliance will enable it to become well-adjusted. Who would have thought that Louise learned a trick, when I could hardly catch her or Ray could not get a leash on her at first? But as our food-motivated Louise sits up for her treat, the new command she must learn is, "Don't take mommy's finger off," as she snatches the goody and slams down her jaws like the snapping of an alligator.

Looking back at these silly capers of Louise is a blessing. Never in a million years did Ray and I think we would reminisce about her escapades. We've had many trials and tribulations concerning Louise's capabilities. But each new day is full of potential for Louise. Our sense of humor is what got us through the "ruff" times.

Nine years later, our extraordinary efforts for an extreme rescue case have been rewarded. Louise is as happy as we can hope she will ever be, and as close to our hearts as ever, growing closer every day.

As you read the story of Louise in this book and our experiences with her, and when you look at her photo, our hope is that you will fall in love with "our Louise," too.

Beagle Bit

A beagle's expected longevity is 12 – 15 years.

Chapter Nineteen

Reflections on Louise's Impact on My Life

    We all need a sense of humor to get through our tough times. A pessimistic attitude gets you nowhere. An optimistic outlook brings favorable results and change. God doesn't dish out what you can't handle. Out of every negative there comes a positive, things happen for a reason. These are clichés that I suppose have substance and meaning when appropriately applied. Did Louise's escape make me a better person? Did it act as a catalyst for me to write this book? Will her story touch people's hearts?

Life threw me some curve balls during the early years with Louise, I admit, and this story sat in a forgotten file on my computer for over six years. I had major back surgery in 2008. In November of 2009, I rescued Tasha, an emaciated beagle from York (Pennsylvania) SPCA who was three years old and weighed only ten pounds. After extensive medical tests, Tasha suffered from a digestive disorder and had psychological problems with eating. It took months to put weight on Tasha and restore her health. Fostering once again consumed me. We adopted Tasha about a year later into our home, so she is our fourth rescue Cree-gle. In March of 2010, Ray's mother passed away. In September of that same year, skin cancer on my face was removed, luckily with no complications. My mother fell ill in 2009 and 2013 and was hospitalized, but recovered fully both times. Adverse situations took precedence over my writing. When we weren't going through a catastrophe, Ray encouraged me to continue writing my book, the story of Louise.

"Why aren't you working on Louise's story?" he'd ask. "If you don't complete it, you did all that work for nothing."

He was right. I had no excuse not to finish the book, especially with being retired. Yes, I took early retirement in June 2007, after twenty-nine years of being an elementary school teacher. That same year, our daughter, Jessica, moved back home from Orlando, Florida, to Harrisburg, Pennsylvania, and bought a townhouse. No more vacationing at theme parks.

It was time to start a new chapter in my life.

Several new chapters fulfill the days of my life now. Among them, I do office work for Ray part-time at our welding business, I volunteer at my local food bank, and Ray and I became first time grandparents in October of 2014. Tanner Ray, a beautiful baby boy, was born to Alicia and her husband, Chris.

In the summer of 2014, a third-grade student I had previously taught invited me to his high school graduation party. His parents were tickled pink that I would attend. I surprised my former student by my appearance. The now eighteen-year-old stood 6'4". A few days later, he wrote me the nicest thank you card, stating how I taught him "that he could be anything he wanted to be if he put his mind to it." Those words affected me deeply and spurred my completion of this book.

Sadly, as I sit at my computer typing Louise's script, I glance over at our Riley, our first foster dog in 2002. Remember the little bugaboo he was when I rescued him from Sally's garage? Our beloved Riley is now twelve and a half years old and is battling an aggressive mast cell skin cancer, which will eventually spread through his body. Good Hope Animal Hospital, Mechanicsburg, Pennsylvania, where Louise fled from, is treating him. Dr. Rob Heidecker can still recall that day in 2006 when Louise's escape disrupted the equilibrium in his office. Today we chuckle about that, but we also are dismayed about Riley's prognosis. Prescribed medications are not slowing down the cancer. We've done multiple surgeries to remove the tumors, but new ones keep appearing. So far he is eating and functional, but it will be hard "when it is time." It always is, and always will be, difficult to say good-bye.

On another somber note, it is probably time to let you, the reader, know that Thelma, Louise's sister, was eventually humanely euthanized. Catherine, her foster mom, was heartbroken she could not help Thelma. Decisions like this are rare in rescue and not made lightly. All avenues of support are explored, medical and behavioral. All possibilities and solutions are exhausted, and a joint effort/team collaboration is made. I contemplated fostering Thelma that summer of 2006, after Louise's escape, so I could have more one-on-one time to rehabilitate her. But Terri, our Furry Friends Network dog trainer, warned that Louise would most likely regress and it was better to keep the sisters separated. Down deep, I knew that Thelma's extreme issues were even too much for me, the Beagle Lady, to handle. And compared to Thelma's lack of progress, I could not risk losing the positive headway made by her sister, Louise. Thelma's heartworm, in and of itself, is an insidious disease. Not to mention her unhinged mind, which provoked biting.

It is sad when a foster dog cannot be rehabilitated, but it can happen.

Another update in the writing of this book and through recommunicating with Catherine, I learned that she relocated to another state and continues her work in rescue. She now concentrates on saving kittens from her local shelter. Despite the geographical distance between us, I feel a strong bond and connection to her because of our foster dogs, Thelma and Louise. I was the lucky one with fostering Louise.

Speaking of rehabilitating accomplishments with Louise, I think back to the maladaptive behavior she exhibited the first few years of fostering and then becoming a Cree-gle at our home. When company came, you remember as I described it in this book, Louise took off with the speed of a roadrunner. Her quaking body showed visible stress at the presence of strangers. She wouldn't be in the same room with our visitors. She panted and paced until they left.

Fast forward today, nine years later. When the doorbell rings, my dogs bark and welcome our company as though these visitors were soldiers just returning from the battlefield. Riley jumps up and down like a pogo stick. BuddyLee does a twinkle toe tap dance on his hind legs. Tasha's aria of howls doesn't frighten anyone. And Louise follows suit in this hero's welcome, always last in line, on two legs pedaling her front paws in the air like she is climbing the rungs of a ladder. Although she remains cautious, she demonstrates suppressed eagerness and now at least seems to be happy seeing people enter our home.

With a houseful of relatives chatting, Louise is not fraught with fear. Teetering her anxiety of people versus her curiosity, she takes precarious steps towards them and gets a quick whiff of their extended hand. So far, the same confidence she shows on the walks has not spilled over into our living room. But she does not run in the other direction as she once did. As I goad her, there have been several people who've been able to pet Louise inside our house. They consider themselves the "elite group." The few. The proud. The "Louise crowd"! Never in a million years did they expect to ever touch Louise. Just the other day, Louise approached my friend Stephanie Willow and received a tender pat on the head. And for some unknown reason, Louise actually cuddles with Ray's thirteen-year-old nephew, Liam Peterson, on the couch. By the looks on their faces, you'd think they won the showcase prize on *The Price Is Right!*

And you should see the broad grin on the face of my mailman, Rick Serbell, as he tosses biscuits from his mail truck to my beagles when they are out in the yard. He claims our house is the favorite on his route as he watches Louise gobble the goodies. Louise emanates a fascination unlike my other beagles. Visiting Louise makes his day!

Louise has gained local notoriety and has a legion of admirers. She has adhered to the hearts of many. Our once epitome-of-fear beagle now walks with an air of nobility on our block. My furry companion paves the way for neighborly relationships so that when they chat with me she does not take off with turbo speed as they approach her. Years of walking has exuded conversations and built close rapport and friendships. My neighbors have now become my extended family, thanks to Louise.

Louise is somewhat of a celebrity in our extended family. When relatives and friends call us, they don't ask how *we're* doing. They ask, "How's that little Louise doing? Think I'll be able to pet her next time I come over?"

I respond with, "Of course you can try. Now, don't you want to hear how my latest back surgery went?"

Louise is infectious. Although she does not display affection for people in the usual dog actions, her grip on everyone's emotions is intoxicating. She hasn't ever licked anyone, jumped on their lap, or let them hold her. But anyone who has ever met her always asks, "How's that little scared beagle of yours? Is she getting better?" She casts some kind of mesmerizing enchantment inside everyone's heart. Maybe she attracts pity, or sympathy. She lures you in with that look in her topaz eyes and those big pupils. She brings out the humanity in us all. We feel her pain. We sense her despair. We wonder what was done to her in her early life to cause all of this fear. Enthralled with her afflictions, we search for answers to understand her distress. And we want to make it right.

I've never experienced a closeness with a dog like I do with Louise. Crossing the inter-species barrier, I feel that Louise and I are kindred souls. Our bond pieces us together like caulking around a window, strengthening the seal and keeping out the harsh elements. In spite of her social ineptness, my love for her is pure, unqualified, unconditional and absolute. In spite of her frailties, I love Louise deeper and different than any of my other beagles. Tracey C. Jones, author of *True Blue leadership: Top 10 Tricks From the Chief Motivational Hound, by Mr. Blue*, refers to this as your "soul dog." The right dog coming at the right place at the right time in your life, that "life-changer" dog.

Louise changed my life, for sure. Ray and I jest that we have two lives, one life *before* and one life *after* Louise. She internally shifted our home. When Louise was not yet with us, things were much easier. I had time for me. We owned normal dogs. Dog droppings could stay in the yard for a day. When company arrived, we didn't have to check the bedroom carpeting for wet spots. We could get up off the couch and not fuss if the static electricity from the acrylic throw blanket frightened Louise. Going away was not a fiasco. Today it is more complicated getting a dog sitter. We must clean up after the dogs more efficiently. Worrying when we're out shopping in a thunderstorm, we rush home to comfort Louise. For many years, we found ourselves apologizing to Louise if we dropped a dish, slammed a cupboard door, or swatted a fly.

I muse what our life would be like without Louise. But there would not have been her escape, no being totally distraught, no lessons of endearment. Louise provides a cornerstone and a fabric that mends us. This canine core component cemented our marriage.

In my junction with Furry Friends Network, I am known as the "Beagle Lady". But now my title is redefined. I am also referred to as "Louise's Mom." "You're the rescuer all those emails were about," people comment. Or "You're the one who got that little scared beagle back. I could not have done what you did." Through this, I have often unpeeled the layers of my psyche, examining my principles, my convictions, my beliefs. With all I did and continue to do for Louise, I give myself a pat on the back for a job well done.

Louise taught me patience, perseverance, and persistence. This special-needs dog opened my eyes and allowed me to look into myself, discovering qualities I didn't know I possessed. At times through my life, I doubt myself, thinking I am not good enough or not capable of a task. I've always tried my best, but sometimes have a doubting inner drive that I could be better. Then, better is never good enough. I have a deep-rooted sense of inadequacy. One time after a classroom observation, my principal commented that I put too much pressure on myself. The old, "I'm my own worst enemy," type of constructive criticism. But, even with her positive comment, I still wondered, was my geography lesson satisfactory for her? Or, did my colleagues like my presentation on reading strategies? Do my school parents think I'm a good teacher? Is my writing good…or does my writing stink? Louise brought out the self-assurance that I was unaware I had.

Louise also showed me that my husband, Ray, an ostensible hard worker and decent man, had the hidden drive and determination to find her when she escaped, too. His commitment to her far surpassed the expectation of an ordinary foster dad. When I was distraught and could not handle the emotional aspect of her disappearance, Ray kept me going, comforted me, invigorated me, gave me hope. He was my hero and he still is. Little does Louise know her escape instilled cohesiveness between us and strengthened our union.

When Louise was missing, my students saw their teacher tired, upset, and distracted. For almost three weeks, my teaching was not at its best. (There I go again, being hard on myself!) But I hope this temporary situation had a greater meaning on their young lives. Perhaps it showed them that tenacity and responsibility pay off, that my love for this animal had a profound purpose and made an impact on their impressionable minds. One thing I know for sure, that class of third grade students will all always remember Louise, her escape and then recovery, for the rest of their lives.

When you reach out and help, whether it be two-legged or four-legged, it builds your confidence and character. You forget about your own shortcomings and become empowered from overcoming obstacles of others. It does every part of you a world of good.

You measure your success not by income, a big house, or a fancy car, but by intrinsic goals that give you a sense of pride, purposefulness, and accomplishment.

I no longer question Louise's being and whether she is happy. I now know Louise was put here with us for a reason. She functions in our house and is content. Our home is her sanctuary.

Every day I look at Louise and relish our days together. Now at age twelve, her nutmeg brown fur has faded to grayish white on her face and eyebrows. Her hearing is diminishing, and she spends a good part of her day sleeping. Every day I look at my fosters and reflect on these amazing dogs. Despite the adversities they've suffered in life, their unconditional love and gratitude have taught me to be a better person and transformed my inner self. Every day I think of Shelley, our early rescue dog that I write about in the beginning of this book, and hope that she knew she was loved and will never be forgotten, even though we only had her with us as a foster for ten days. Shelley will live on through this book. Then I look at my Louise, and honestly don't know whether to laugh or cry, or maybe some of both, but I am sure grateful she was placed in my hands for her care.

Louise came to me on that wintry day in late 2005 as vulnerable as a baby bird that needed to leave the nest and face the world. Little by little, we celebrate her evolution from a deeply troubled dog to an ongoing success story. I commemorate my feelings from insufficiency to ovation, all because of a beagle I am smitten with. I will continue to raise the bar with Louise, push her limits, and not give up on a disturbed dog. She may never be a plucky pet or possess the same hospitality skills as a therapy dog, but we commend her minute milestones. She's come a long way from that hog pen in the snow in West Virginia to enjoying her existence as a Cree-gle.

By the way, Louise says "Hi"…(for now) from a distance.

And she adds, "Thank you for joining me on my journey!"

Beagle Bit

The Westminster Dog Show began in 1877. It took 132 years for a beagle to win Best in Show. A 15 inch beagle, "Uno," claimed the title in 2008. "Uno" was the first Best in Show winner ever to be invited to the White House for a visit. In 2015, breed history repeated itself. A beagle named "Miss P" won the Westminster Dog Show Best in Show.

My Life in Rescue Work with Furry Friends Network

by Sharon Cree, Author

Furry Friends Network, located in central Pennsylvania, founded in 2001, is a non-profit organization that is strictly dedicated to "rescue and foster" work. It is not a shelter. Two sisters-in-law run Furry Friends Network…Robin Scherer, who is the co-founder and executive director in charge of the dogs and Shawna Scherer, co-founder, who is the rescue's cat lady.

Furry Friends Network, *furryfriendsnetwork.com*, operates entirely with volunteers fostering dogs and cats in their residences. In order to adopt a dog or cat that volunteers have fostered, there is a stringent application process and home visits are performed to ensure a successful adoption. It's important every time to match the right owner to the right pet. Foster animals are fully vetted receiving their shots, heartworm test, and flea and tick preventative. Foster pets are micro-chipped, fixed, and also receive any other medical care deemed necessary. If you adopt from the Furry Friends Network, there are certain expectations, such as a dog must attend obedience school and a cat must be kept inside your home. A lifelong partnership is formed. Spay/neuter philosophy is mandatory to control the pet overpopulation problem in this country.

I have the utmost respect, admiration and love for these two women who founded and now operate Furry Friends Network. To be honest, rescue work can consume you. Along with the hard work are happy stories of adoption, but there are also challenges.

Dealing with sick and injured animals, paying medical bills, handling behavioral issues, working full-time jobs, answering what can add up to hundreds of emails per day, processing applications and handling successful adoptions are some of the many duties that accompany a successful rescue operation. The expense is staggering; fundraising is critical to any rescue's existence. To those of us who give a part of our life to rescue work, it is a passion with many rewards.

In my thirteen years with Furry Friends Network, I've fostered about fifty beagles. "Beagle Lady" is my official, or non-official, title within the rescue. This name was bestowed on me by Stephanie Grossnickle, whose house becomes the foster home for many of the larger breeds, especially hounds. I am proud to answer to that title. I love beagles!

Beagles are a small and friendly breed. Beagles make good family pets. Many are unwanted because either they do not hunt the way the owners want them to hunt, or they are gun shy. If they are not good hunters, they are often considered "worthless" and of "no use." Some beagles are skittish. I enjoy working with them and getting them to come out of their shell, nurturing them to their highest potential…a warm and loving companion pet. When a beagle gets adopted, it is rewarding to see him or her live the life the dog should have had in the first place. I find it immensely gratifying and I'm always happy for that beagle to find its forever home. This is one of the rewards of foster and rescue work.

Rescue dogs are amazingly resilient to the injustices man has done to them. One of my foster beagles, Paige, was a cruelty case. She limped for eight months and walked with an exaggerated gait. We consulted an orthopedic vet in hopes of helping her to walk properly again. Despite our best efforts, her leg had to be amputated. However, Paige was one friendly, energetic, "three-legged pooch!" Nothing slowed her down!

Another beagle, Oakley, was dumped in a night pen at a shelter. He was lucky to have survived and spent three weeks in an animal hospital from injuries sustained that night from other dogs in that night pen. Ray and I bandaged Oakley's wounds for two months. We poured honey treatments over his skin to aid the healing process.

Both Paige and Oakley are a testament to courage and valor. They endured much pain and suffering through their ordeals, yet were never mean or snappy to us. Both Paige and Oakley were adopted and are happily in their forever homes, or as we like to say in rescue work, their *"fur-ever"* homes! Their bravery humbles me every time I think about them. It was an honor to have these dogs as part of my life.

Once in a great while I venture out of my rescue "beagle box." Wyatt, a four-month-old Golden Retriever/Great Pyrenees mix, was fostered by me. Wyatt was adopted and then returned to the shelter in West Virginia because the wife did not want a dog. Wyatt then arrived through a transport to Furry Friends Network and that's when I fostered him. Wyatt looked like a golden fluffy puff-ball! My neighbors commented on how beautiful he was.

Wyatt had the worst case of kennel cough I had ever encountered when I fostered him. Many times I put him in our bathroom and ran the shower so that the steam could break up his congestion. He was sick for three weeks. Once he was healthy, Wyatt was adopted by a loving couple. And, there is a happy twist to Wyatt's story! A year and a half after he was adopted, Wyatt saved their lives! Their home caught fire in the middle of the night. Wyatt barked and growled incessantly, like he had never done before, to awaken them. Wyatt saved them and was a hero! That is invaluable and one of many good stories about our rescued and adopted pets!

Many people ask me, "How can you be a foster home for pets, Sharon?" and also "How can you give them up? Don't you get too attached?"

There is a thorough application process. References are called and a phone interview is conducted. I perform many of my foster dog's home visits to inspect the premises to safeguard a proper environment. Throughout this process, I become well-acquainted with the applicant, making it easier to "let the foster go." We as fosters to these dogs and cats know that each will find a suitable match with their new owner. Furry Friends Network wants to guarantee a permanent home for each animal in our care. That makes it easier to "give them up," knowing they are being placed in a good home. At that point, our foster work with that particular dog or cat is complete.

I keep in touch with many of the families who have adopted beagles that I have fostered from Furry Friends Network. We have become friends. I enjoy receiving updates and emails about my foster dogs' new chances at life in forever homes with their new loving families. Often, I feel like all of my hard work and devotion pays off, especially when I hear favorable stories.

"Thanks for all that you've done, Sharon" is music to my ears and warms my heart… *every time!*

"Our new dog has brought great joy into our life" is the comment made by many of the families that have adopted "my beagles."

I look at it this way: I am the stepping stone and the middle person between the dog finding a new and happier life and a family finding a loving companion pet.

Of course, when one foster dog gets adopted, there are others to save. It goes on and on.

Letter from Dolly, a Foster Beagle, on Her Way to Her New Forever Home

Hi, New Mommy and Daddy!

Foster Mom Sharon was very sad today. She moped around the house. I wasn't naughty, was I?

Then she finally sat me down, petted me lovingly and said, "Dolly, we need to have a little talk. Tomorrow you are getting adopted. You will go to your forever home. These nice people will love you and take care of you the rest of your life. My job is done."

And then she packed some toys and treats for me like I was going on vacation! So I will see you at the Carlisle pet adoption center at 6:00 p.m.

Please tell my new big sister, Maya, to save me space on the couch.

Love,
    Dolly

Beagle Bit

Snoopy made his debut on October 2, 1950.

Saving lives, one animal at a time.

A Message from Furry Friends Network Co-Founder, Robin Scherer

In the 1970s, American shelters euthanized from between 12 and 20 million dogs and cats, at a time when there were 67 million pets in homes. Today, shelters euthanize around 4 million animals, while there are more than 135 million dogs and cats in homes. This enormous decline in euthanasia numbers—from around 25% of American dogs and cats euthanized every year to about 3%—represents substantial progress.

We will make still greater progress by working together to strike at the roots of animal overpopulation through overbreeding and lack of spaying and neutering. Thanks to foster parents like Sharon Cree, Furry Friends Network's resident "Beagle Lady" and the author of this book, and other foster parents like her, rescues and shelters are able to save more animals from being victims of the gross overpopulation problem that continues to exist in our communities.

There is always more work to be done, always more dogs and cats that need help. The work is overwhelming and challenging, like saving Louise, the scared rescue beagle in this book, but it is always worth the efforts we make. Saving a dog or cat's life is priceless!

For all pet owners who adopt a rescue dog or cat, or any pet, we salute you, we thank you, and we encourage others to do the same. You are saving an animal's life…and, they are adding great enjoyment to yours!

Robin Sch

Robin Scherer

Co-Founder & Executive Director, Furry Friends Network

Founded in 2001, Furry Friends Network is a non-profit, all-volunteer animal adoption organization based in central Pennsylvania. Furry Friends Network is not a shelter, but instead uses a foster home network to house the rescue animals until permanent, indoor homes can be found, offering second chances at lifetimes of love and happiness.

www.furryfriendsnetwork.com

Furry Friends Network Facts

More than 6,000 companion animals have been given a new "leash" on life because of Furry Friends Network.

Last year, our dedicated volunteers were able to save 295 dogs - placing 225 of them in forever homes and 70 in foster care awaiting their adoptive homes. In addition, 238 cats were brought into foster care, with 186 adopted by permanent, loving families and 52 residing in foster care until their permanent adoptive homes are found. We are proud of our accomplishments but these statistics are not just numbers to us. These are loving, affectionate companion animals with no voice to advocate for themselves.

Our Furry Friends Network members consider it an honor and a calling to give voices to these helpless animals. We are all committed to not only finding loving, forever homes for these animals, but to also getting them all the appropriate medical care they need prior to adoption. Veterinary expenses - paid entirely by Furry Friends Network - totaled $123,110 last year. Furry Friends Network also covers all rescue-related expenses such as transportation, crates, collars, leashes and food.

We need your help to continue our mission. Please find a place in your heart to help these unconditionally loving animals who have done nothing to deserve the wretched treatment so many have endured. Your tax-free charitable gift - of any amount - will help Furry Friends Network with our cause.

Thank you!
Warm Regards,

Robin S/L

Robin Scherer
Co-Founder & Executive Director, Furry Friends Network

Furry Friends Network
P.O. Box 519
Boiling Springs, PA 17007

www.furryfriendsnetwork.com

    Furry Friends Network is an all-volunteer non-profit organization. We have no paid staff and rely exclusively on loving foster homes to save dogs and cats in need. Our dedicated and caring volunteers take in animals from shelters, neglectful and abusive environments, strays and owner-surrendered animals. Without Furry Friends Network, these dogs and cats would be euthanized or die alone without knowing the kindness of a human.

    All Furry Friends Network animals receive crucial medical care prior to being adopted. Specifically, foster dogs receive an annual exam, spay/neuter, rabies, bordatella, and distemper vaccines, dewormer, microchip ID, annual tests for heartworm/lyme/ erlichia/anaplasmosis and receive monthly flea/tick and heartworm preventative. Furry Friends Network cats receive an annual exam, spay/neuter, rabies and distemper vaccines, microchip ID, feline leukemia/FIV test, dewormer, and flea/tick preventative.

    The official registration and financial information of Furry Friends Network may be obtained from the Pennsylvania Department of State by calling toll free, within Pennsylvania, 1 (800) 732-0999. Registration does not imply endorsement.

Rescue and Shelter Facts

- 96% of dogs surrendered at a shelter have never attended obedience school.

- It is estimated that 1 in 5 pets gets lost in their lifetime. Make sure your cat or dog wears an ID tag and is micro-chipped.

- Black dogs are the first to get euthanized and the last to get adopted. This is called "Black Dog Syndrome."

- In 6 years, one unspayed female dog and her offspring can reproduce 67,000 dogs.

- Only 10 – 20% of cats and dogs are adopted from shelters and rescues.

- Only 1 out of every 10 dogs ever finds a permanent home. Only 1 out of 12 cats ever finds its permanent home.

- Eight million dogs and cats enter shelters each year. More than half won't make it out alive.

- Approximately 25% of dogs taken to shelters are purebreds.

- Foreclosure and moving are topping the list right now of reasons an owner may surrender a pet. Closely related, a landlord not allowing a pet on the premises is the second reason for relinquishing a pet.

- Each day 10,000 humans are born in the U.S. Each day 70,000 puppies and kittens are born. As long as these birth rates exist, there will never be enough homes for all the animals.

- There are 70 million stray dogs and cats living in the U.S.

- Only 10% of animals received by shelters have been spayed or neutered.

- There are 164 million pet dogs and cats in the U.S. One in 20 will end up in a shelter by the end of the year.

Bibliography

ANIMAL WELFARE GROUPS AND RESCUE ORGANIZATIONS:

American Humane Association (AHA)
1400 16th Street NW, Suite 360
Washington, D.C. 20036
www.americanhumane.org

American Society for the Prevention of Cruelty to Animals (ASPCA)
424 East 92nd Street
New York, NY 10128-6804
www.aspca.org

AngelPets.org
P.O. Box 236
Dauphin, PA 17018-0236
Telephone: (717) 921-2117

Beagle Freedom Project
4804 Laurel Canyon Boulevard, #534
Valley Village, CA 91607
www.beaglefreedomproject.org

Central Pennsylvania Animal Alliance
180 Walden Way
Mechanicsburg, PA 17050
www.cpaa.info

Furry Friends Network
P.O. Box 519
Boiling Springs, PA 17007
www.furryfriendsnetwork.com

The Humane Society of the United States (HSUS)
2100 L Street NW
Washington, D.C. 20037
www.hsus.org

Humane Society of Harrisburg Area
7790 Grayson Road
Harrisburg, PA 17111
www.humanesocietyhbg.org

INTERNET RESOURCES:

www.beagle-facts.com
www.beaglepro.com
www.beaglesunlimited.com
www.beagles-on-the-web.com
www.blackdogrescueproject.org
www.brewbeagles.com
www.dogbreedinfo.com

www.dogchannel.com
www.mybeagletraining.com
www.petpopulation.org
www.spayusa.org
www.thedogrescuers.com
www.ttouch.com
www.welovebeagles.com

BOOKS:

Greye, Jan and Smith, Gail. *Puppy Parenting.* HarperCollins Publishers. NY. 2001

Grogan, John. *Marley & Me, The world's worst dog will bring out the best in their family.* HarperCollins Publishers. New York, NY 2005

Jones, Tracey C. *True Blue Leadership: Top 10 Tricks from the Chief Motivational Hound.* Tremendous Life Books. Mechanicsburg, PA. 2011

McLennan, Bardi. *Rescue Me.* Kennel Club Books. NJ. 2007

Millan, Cesar and Peltier, Melissa Jo. *Cesar's Way, The Natural, Everyday Guide to Understanding & Correcting Common Dog Problems.* Harmony Books. New York. 2006

Millan, Cesar and Peltier, Melissa Jo. *Cesar's Rules: Your Way to Train a Well-Behaved Dog.* Crown Publishing. New York. 2010

Millan, Cesar. *Short Guide to a Happy Dog, 98 Essential Tips and Techniques.* National Geographic Society. Washington, D.C. 2013

Moore, Arden. *What Dogs Want.* Firefly Books Ltd. NY. 2012

Morgan, Diane and Hunthausen, Wayne, DVM. *The Beagle.* T.F.H. Publications, Inc. Neptune City, NJ. 2005

Robertson, Julia. *The Complete Dog Massage Manual.* Velace Publishing Limited. England. 2010

Roth, Richard. *The Beagle.* Howell Book House, NY, NY. 1996

Sternberg, Sue. *Successful Dog Adoption.* Howell Book House. Indianapolis, Indiana. 2003

MAGAZINES:

Healthy Pet. Douglas Drew, Publisher. Summer 2008

ORGANIZATIONS:

American Kennel Club
5580 Centerview Drive
Raleigh, NC 27606
www.akc.org

OTHER RESOURCES:

National Council on Pet Population Study & Policy, Shelter Statistics Survey

PAMPHLETS:

Pet Kardlets™ *Beagle.* Seek Publishing. Millersville, TN

TRAINER:

Terri Bullers
Canine Behavior Clinic
Mechanicsburg, PA 17050
Email: doghelpfast@gmail.com
www.k9behaviorclinic.com

About the Author

Sharon Tynio Cree grew up in Harrisburg, Pennsylvania. Sharon's family's roots stem from the coal regions of Pennsylvania. She has fond memories of spending a few weeks each summer with cousins in the anthracite-mining town of Frackville.

As a teenager, Sharon babysat and saved money to take a trip to Europe when she was sixteen. She toured nine countries, from Greece to England. Sharon still loves to travel!

Sharon had two dogs growing up: one, a black and white terrier named Chi Chi, and the other, a purebred Siberian Husky named Nikki. Her love of beagles started when she was in college and bought a beagle named Barney at a local shelter. A move to the college campus to continue her degree brought restrictions against having a dog live with her. This tough decision led to Sharon having to find a good home for Barney. She stayed in touch with the new owners and visited often. Barney turned out to be quite a character, a trait that Sharon continues to love about the beagle breed, their colorful personalities.

Sharon earned her teaching degree from Penn State Middletown campus and taught elementary school. Her job position included first, second, and third graders in the same school district that she attended as a young girl. She taught in that school district for twenty-nine years, finally retiring in 2007.

A call from her sister, Denise, a dog groomer, and also an animal lover, in 2002, introduced Sharon to the world of "rescue." Both Sharon and Denise volunteer for the Furry Friends Network rescue organization in central Pennsylvania. Sharon has earned the name "Beagle Lady" within the organization. She has fostered and placed over 50 beagles to good homes. Her work as a foster mother to mostly beagles continues to this day.

Louise, the subject of this book, is a "one of a kind" beagle, the "most scared dog in the world." Louise's photo on the Internet on Sharon's computer tugged at her heart, and so the adventure began! Louise finally arrived to Furry Friends Network in Pennsylvania in a transport from a shelter in West Virginia in late December 2005. Sharon's dedicated efforts to rehabilitate Louise were not working. Louise was even afraid of bacon frying on the stove! Then, in a freak incident, Louise got loose outside at a vet's office, nearby one of the busiest highways and business locations in the area! Frustration ensued as Sharon and her husband, Ray, searched for Louise high and low, day and night, for several weeks. You'll just have to read the book for the rest of this amazing story.

"Beagle-mania" continues at the Cree household with their "Cree-gles," what they call their own beagles, and fosters who come and then go to their forever homes.

Sharon and her husband, Ray, and several beagles including Louise, live in Dauphin, Pennsylvania. Their two daughters, Jessica and Alicia, are grown and also live in the area. In October 2014, Sharon and Ray became grandparents to Tanner Ray, son of Alicia and her husband, Chris.

In addition to her foster and rescue work, Sharon also enjoys fundraising for Furry Friends Network, baking, walking, reading, and volunteering at her local food bank.